Landscapes of
MENORCA

a countryside guide
Fifth edition

Rodney Ansell

Fifth edition © 2010
Sunflower Books™
PO Box 36160
Lond
www

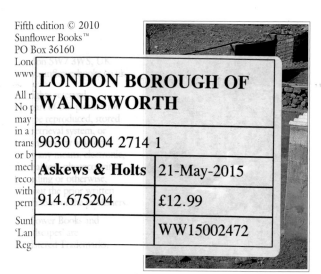

ISBN 978-1-85691-376-8

At Sant Patrici (Walk 14)

Important note to the reader

We have tried to ensure that the descriptions and maps in this book are error-free at press date. The book will be updated, where necessary, whenever future printings permit. It will be very helpful for us to receive your comments (sent in care of the publishers, please) for the updating of future printings.

    We also rely on those who use this book — especially walkers — to take along a good supply of common sense when they explore. While walls and gates enclosing private land cause the most problems for walkers on the island (see the article on page 42), *storm damage may make a route unsafe at any time*. If the route is not as we outline it here, and your way ahead is not secure, return to the point of departure. *Never attempt to complete a tour or walk under hazardous conditions!* Please read carefully the country code on page 10, the walking notes on pages 30 and 31, and the introductory comments at the beginning of each tour and walk (regarding road conditions, equipment, grade, distances and time, etc). Explore *safely*, while at the same time respecting the beauty of the countryside.

Cover photograph: Cala Macarella (Walks 17, 18 and 19)
Title page: Talatí de Dalt (Picnic 5; Car tour 2; Walks 7 and 8)

Photographs by the author, except for pages 33, 39, 53, 98 (Hans Losse)
    and page 104 and cover (shutterstock)
Maps by the author and Sunflower Books, based on Spanish military maps
    (with kind permission of the Servicio Geográfico del Ejército)
Drawings by John Theasby
A CIP catalogue record for this book is available from the British Library.
Printed and bound in China: W K T Company Ltd

● Contents

Ploughing with a donkey near Sant Lluís (Car tour 1, Walk 12)

SOME FEATURES OF THE MENORCAN LANDSCAPE

Preface

Menorca is the island people fall in love with ... the one they go back to year after year, the island where they go to retire. And no wonder. For in addition to all the normal attractions you expect from a holiday island — lively resorts, good safe beaches, day-long sunshine, splendid restaurants — Menorca has something special. Such as dozens of lovely untouched beaches and a gorgeous countryside. And, as if that were not enough, it has the densest concentration of prehistoric monuments in Europe.

Although only small, much of the island is isolated and, without the help this book provides, difficult for the visitor to penetrate. Two days' motoring will enable you to see most of that part of the island which is accessible by car (by no means all of it). As for the rest, it is gentle walking country and the remoter regions are best explored on foot — or by bicycle.

Acknowledgements

My thanks to the following people, who have helped me with the preparation of the material for this book:

Señora María Angeles Hernandez Gómez, Cronista Arxivera Municipal of Mahón, and her colleagues in the Ajuntament, for advice on rights of way (and suggesting Walk 2); Señor Lorenzo Cavallir of the Department of Works of the Consell Insular; Sr Rafael Valls, Legal Attaché at the Spanish Embassy in London, for his advice on Spanish law; Alan Goodin, for his help with the island's flora and birds; Frankie and John Cross, who not only drew on many years' familiarity with (and love of) Menorca to advise me, but also found out and brought back all those things I had overlooked. Very special thanks to my wife, Helen, for her constant encouragement and readiness to act as guinea-pig, and to my publishers for help with updating this edition. Finally, to the many people who have written to me with information and suggestions, several of which have been included.

Useful books

Your library or local bookshop can suggest the best general guides, prior to your departure. When you are on the island, you should be able to find the following useful reference books: Joan Montserrat, Jaume Serrat *et al*, *Guide Menorca;* Hoskin and Waldren, *Taulas and Talayots;* Rev Fernando Marti, *History of Menorca;* M G Barredo, *Flowers of Menorca* and R Escandrell and S Catchot, *Birds of Menorca;* both can be purchased at the GOB bookshops in Mahón (59 Camí d'Es Castell) and Ciutadella (38 Camí de Maó, only open Tuesdays 09.00-13.00 and Thursdays 10.00-14.00 and 17.00-20.00).

If you enjoy using this book, and you would like to explore the countryside on another Balearic Island, Sunflower also publishes *Landscapes of Mallorca* and *Landscapes of Ibiza and Formentera* available from your local library or bookshop.

Introduction

How to get there

Menorca is easily reached by air to Mahón airport. From May to October package holidays and 'flight only' arrangements from various airports throughout the UK are plentiful. There are also some scheduled flights all year round — for instance with Monarch Airlines out of London Luton, Gatwick, Birmingham or Manchester.

Geography

The island is small — only some 50 kilometres (30 miles) by 20 kilometres (12 miles) at its widest point. It is also a fairly flat island. There are low hills in the north, but there are no mountains. At 358m (1175ft), Monte Toro, in the centre of the island, is the highest point. This makes for easy walking.

The most significant geographical feature is the *cala*, the creek or fjord terminating in a tiny sandy beach. These lie at the end of the ravines, or *barrancs*, which cut through the southern half of the island particularly. Because of the many *barrancs,* the basic road pattern of Menorca is a central highway (the Me-1), from which arms branch off to the various beach resorts (*urbanizaciones*). There is no motorable coastal road round the island, and circular drives are difficult to plan. (But there *is* a 'coastal road' for *walkers* — see page 100.)

The vast majority of the population lives in five towns (Mahón, Alaior, Es Mercadal, Ferreries and Ciutadella) strung across the centre of the island along the Me-1. Holidaymakers generally stay in a number of resorts dotted around the coast, mostly in the south and west. The rest of the island is given over to isolated farms, which connect with the road system and each other by rough tracks and, increasingly, newly-surfaced lanes — the setting for most of the walks suggested in this book. The fields, mostly used for dairy cattle, are separated by drystone walls, and sometimes, if you do any of the walks, you will be called upon to scale them. In some cases, protruding stones (*botadores*) help you over these hurdles. (It should not be difficult to climb over the walls on any of the walks in this book.)

Weather

July and August are hot and sunny. While there will be the occasional overcast or windy day, these will be infrequent. During spring, early summer and autumn, expect more cloudy days and rain. Menorca is the wettest of the Balearic Islands. It is the price paid for its gorgeous vegetation and abundant bird life. But it will not be cold, and there will be many hot and sunny days as well. A feature of the winter months is a strong, sometimes quite cold wind which at times blows from the north.

If you go to Menorca hoping to do some walking, the overcast days are a bonus — it is far more enjoyable walking then than in full sunshine. Again, provided you have adequate protective clothing, the walks described here are an excellent alternative to paperback novels or gin rummy as a way of dealing with those wet days.

Where to stay

The bulk of the holiday accommodation is to be found in the beach resorts. There are plenty of hotels and apartments. Many people also stay in holiday villas. There is a shortage of domestic help: the population is small and fully employed. You will look in vain for signs of poverty. Hardly any accommodation is available between November and April. The exceptions would be the Hotel Alfonso III in Ciutadella and some small *hostales* in Mahón. There are campsites at Es Clot and Torre Solí-Nou (see the touring map).

Getting about on the island

A frequent **bus service** plies between Mahón and Ciutadella along the Me-1, calling at the three intervening towns where there are bus stops *(paradas fijas)* whose locations change regularly. The bus leaves Mahón from Avinguda J A Clavé, near the Plaça de S'Esplanada, and Ciutadella from the Plaça dels Pins, south of the Plaça de S'Esplanada. A less frequent service goes from Mahón to Fornells via Arenal and Son Parc. The services to the beach resorts only operate in the summer. These link the southern resorts with Mahón, and the northwestern ones with Ciutadella. Bus timetables are given on pages 133-134. Don't rely solely on these, however. As soon as you arrive on the island, update these timetables by getting 'first-hand' information from the bus stations mentioned above, the tourist offices, or the bus stops. Buses generally run to time but, to be on the safe side, always arrive about ten minutes early. Most of the walks described in this book can be reached by bus. Not all walks will be convenient from your resort, but there will be some that are. A few walks can only be reached by car.

Taxis are only a phone call away should you miss your bus. If you can use your mobile phone to make local calls in Menorca, you can use a **taxi** to get to the start of a walk and arrange where to be picked up when you call at the end of the walk. This enables you to do all those walks described as 'only accessible by car'.

Your holiday rep, hotel reception and the tourist information offices in Ciutadella and Mahón can all provide you with telephone numbers. The Associació Menorquina Radio-taxi operates a 24 hour service. The number is 971 36 71 11. All fares should be ascertained in advance.

The package tour couriers arrange **coach tours** which get you to all the tourist points of interest, but never off the beaten track.

Boat trips around the coast are also arranged by the tour companies, or can be booked privately from Mahón, Es Castell and Ciutadella harbours. These often provide a barbecue lunch at a beach.

Bicycles can be readily hired, and the countryside south of Ciutadella in particular lends itself to exploration in this way. Information about waymarked cycle trails is available from tourist offices. But be warned: the tarmac roads have a habit of turning into rough tracks — although these are ideal for mountain bikes!

Language hints

In the tourist centres you hardly need know any Spanish. But out in the countryside, a few words of the language will be helpful, especially if you lose your way. Here's an (almost) foolproof way to communicate in Spanish. First, memorise the few short key questions and their possible answers, given below.

Then, when you have your 'mini-speech' memorised, *always ask the many questions you can concoct from it in such a way that you get a 'sí' (yes) or 'no' answer*. Never ask an open-ended question such as 'Where is the main road?' Instead, ask the question and then suggest the most likely answer yourself. For instance: 'Good day, sir. Please — where is the path to Ferreries? Is it straight ahead?' Now, unless you get a 'sí' response, try: 'Is it to the left?'

If you go through the list of answers to your own question, you will eventually get a 'sí' response, and this is more reassuring than relying on sign language.

Following are the most likely situations in which you may have to practise your Spanish. The dots (...) show where you will fill in the name of your destination. Ask a local person — perhaps someone at your hotel — to help you with the pronunciation of place names.

■ Asking the way

Key questions

English	Spanish	Pronunciation
Good day	Buenos días	Boo-**eh**-nohs **dee**-ahs
sir (madam, miss)	señor (señora, señorita)	sen-**yor** (sen-**yor**-ah, sen-yor-**ee**-tah)
Please — where is	Por favor — dónde está	Poor fah-**vor** — **dohn**-day es-**tah**

the road to … ?	la carretera a … ?	lah cah-reh-**teh**-rah ah… ?
the footpath to …?	la senda de … ?	lah **sen**-dah day … ?
the way to … ?	el camino a … ?	el cah-**mee**-noh ah … ?
the bus stop?	la parada?	lah pah-**rah**-dah?
Many thanks.	Muchas gracias.	**Moo**-chas **gra**-thee-ahs.

Possible answers

English	Spanish	Pronunciation
Is it here?	Está aquí?	es-**tah** ah- **kee**?
there?	allí?	ahl-**yee**?
straight ahead?	todo recto?	**toh**-doh **rayk**-toh?
behind?	detrás?	day-**tras**?
right?	a la derecha?	ah lah day-**ray**-chah?
left?	a la izquierda?	ah lah eeth-kee-**er**-dah?
above?	arriba?	ah-**ree**-bah?
below?	abajo?	ah-**bah**-hoh?

- **Asking a taxi driver to take you somewhere and return for you, or asking a taxi to meet you at a certain place and time**

English	Spanish	Pronunciation
Please —	Por favor —	Poor fah-**vor** —
take us to …	llévanos a …	l-**yay**-vah-nohs ah …
and return	y venga buscarnos	ee **vain**-gah boos-**kar**-nohs
at (place) at (time)	a … a …*	ah (place) ah (time)*

*Point out the time on your watch.

Place names

The majority of place names on Menorca are the names of farmhouses. Occasionally you will see the name written large across the façade of the house. Where a settlement of any kind has to be named, from talayotic village to *urbanización*, it invariably takes its name from the farm on whose land it lies.

Generally the names are old. Many go back to the days of the Moors and are in Arabic, but most are Menorquín, the old language of the island, derived from Catalan. Some are in modern Catalan, and a few in Spanish. Do not be surprised to see as many as three or four spellings for the same place — as at the farm of Son Mercer, visited on Walk 15.

A number of words occur again and again, and with the hope that it may add interest to your excursions, I offer below an explanation of the most frequent.

Firstly, however, some pronunciation hints are called for. In Menorquín 'ç' is pronounced as 's', 'll' as 'y' and 'x' as 'sh'. Here again, I do urge you to get some tips on pronunciation from a local person.

---

torre — a tower (sometimes corrupted to *turru* or *torr*). Menorca is full of towers, from prehistoric *talayots* to the watchtowers of the 17th and 18th centuries, by way of the fortified farmhouses of the Middle Ages, and a great many names include this element.

es, sa, ses — Menorquín equivalents of the Spanish *el, la, los/las*. *En, na* are variants of *es* and *sa*, used when referring to people, including proper names. All mean the same: 'the', as does *els* (Catalan) and *al* (Arabic).

san (Spanish), *sant* (Catalan), and *santa* (common to both Spanish and Catalan) mean saint: thus Sant Joan = San Juán = Saint John; Sant Jaume = San Jaime = Saint James.

cova or *cove* — a cave
cala — a creek or cove
barranc(o) — a gorge, river, or valley
son — a large farmhouse
bou — an ox

lloc, lluc — a Moorish word for a farmhouse
bini — a very common Moorish word meaning 'sons'
nou — new
vell (also *vella, vei, vey*) — old
de dalt — higher
de baix — lower
de devant — in front
de derrera — behind

The six above entries are usually found in pairs. As families grew, and the sons built their homes nearby, the new farms were distinguished in this way from the parents' farm.

In recent years there has been a strong revival of the Menorquín language. Many Spanish names of both towns and streets have been altered to Menorquín and/or Catalan, and many of the signs indicating public buildings, etc have also been revised. Some of the most common Menorquín words, with Spanish and English equivalents, follow:

Towns:

Maó — Mahón
Alaior — Alayor
Es Migjorn (Gran) — San Cristobal
Sant Lluís — San Luís

Ciutadella — Ciudadela
Ferreries — Ferrerías
Sant Climent — San Clemente
Es Castell — Villa-Carlos

Streets, etc:

carrer (calle) — street
plaça (plaza) — square
ajuntament (ayuntamiento) — town hall
centre ciutat (centro ciudad) — city centre

costa (cuesta) — hill
avinguda (avenida) — avenue
mercat (mercado) — market
platja (playa) — beach
camí (camino) — road

Shops, etc:

obert (abierto) — open

tancat (cerrado) — closed

The name of the island:

The Romans called it Minorica, from which the English name Minorca was derived. It means the 'smaller' island (Majorca being the larger one). The Spanish equivalents are Menorca and Mallorca.

Country code

Experienced ramblers are used to following a country code; tourists perhaps less so. Please heed the following guidelines during your visit to Menorca.

- Do not light fires.
- Do not frighten animals.
- Walk quietly through all hamlets and villages.
- Leave all gates just as you find them.

Walk 14: cows near Ferreries. Ever since Sir Richard Kane introduced British breeds of cattle, dairy farming has been an important agricultural activity on Menorca.

■ Protect all wild and cultivated plants. Don't try to pick wild flowers or uproot saplings. Fruit and other crops are someone's private property and should not be touched.

■ Never walk over cultivated land (unless there is an explicit instruction to do so in the text, as in Walk 15).

■ Take all your litter away with you.

■ Walkers — Do not take risks! Do not attempt walks beyond your capacity, and do not wander off the paths described here, especially if it is late in the day. **Do not walk alone**, and *always* tell a responsible person exactly where you are going and what time you plan to return. Remember, if you become lost or injure yourself, it may be a long time before you are found. On any but a very short walk close to towns or villages, take some extra food, water, and warm clothing. A torch and whistle, even a compass, might be carried as well. *Do* read the guidelines on grade and equipment for each walk you plan.

PREHISTORIC MONUMENTS

Menorca is home to the greatest concentration of prehistoric monuments on earth. It is only recently that many of them have been excavated, restored, or cleared of the vegetation that for centuries had overwhelmed them. Very many more await excavation. Several of the walks in this book include visits to some of the most interesting of these monuments.

The people of ancient Menorca worked with stone. The island is lacking in commercially useful metal ores, and there are no large trees for timber. Stone on the other hand abounds: south of a line drawn

Talayot *at Talatí de Dalt*

roughly from Cala Morell to Mahón via Ferreries, a young and easily-worked limestone is found, which nevertheless becomes hard and durable when exposed to the atmosphere.

There are five principal kinds of building to be seen: caves, *talayots*, *taulas*, hypostyle chambers and *navetas*.

carefully and skilfully chiselled out of the rock. Later generations moved out of the caves between 1400 and 1000 BC, and for the next thousand years they were used only as burial chambers. While you will see caves on most walks, the best and easiest to explore will be found on Walks 2, 5, 11, 13, 17, 18, 19 and 23 and on Picnics 4, 10, 11, 15, 16 and 18.

Capades de Moro at Cala Morell (Walk 23)

Caves *(illustrated on page 131)*

After 2500 BC the earliest inhabitants carved out caves for themselves to live in. Those who suppose that cavemen were primitive savages inhabiting natural holes in the cliffs will be totally unprepared for the sophisticated craftsmanship of these troglodytic homes, all of which were

Taula *at Trepucó*

Talayots *(illustrated on pages 54-55, 60-61, 79)*

These great conical mounds of stones, 5-10m (15-30ft) high, are very common on the island. Many are solid; some have an inside chamber and passage. All are now truncated. Their original purpose is not known. Many suggestions have been made. Perhaps they had a timber house on top — for the local chieftain. Or they could have been defence towers, farmhouses, or storerooms. They are always associated with settlements. The best *talayots* are seen on Walks 2, 5, 7, 8, 12, 13, 17 and 22 and Picnics 5, 13, 21 and 22.

Taulas (illustrated on pages 1 and 54-55)

Most fascinating are the *taulas*, named from the Latin word *ta(b)ula* meaning 'table'. Whereas the *talayot* is not totally unlike buildings found elsewhere (the *nuraghe* of Sardinia for example), the *taula* is unique to Menorca.

It is a large, sometimes huge, slab of stone, set upright in a groove in the rock and supporting another large slab lying horizontally across it. The *taula* is always found in settlements, never far from a *talayot*, and inside a small horseshoe shaped enclosure, surrounded by standing stones, like a tiny Stonehenge.

Once again, nobody knows what they were for, and the ancient writers do not mention them. It is claimed they are too tall to be altars, and the most popular suggestion is that they are idols, like totem poles in North America, symbols of gods. One scholar has suggested that they may represent bulls' heads.

Most of the best *taulas* on the island are visited during Walks 2, 5, 7, 8 and 17 or Picnics 5, 13 and 22.

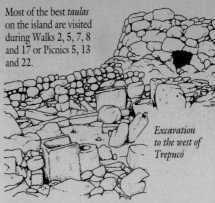

Excavation to the west of Trepucó

Hypostyle chambers (illustrated below)

'Hypostyle chamber' describes a roof supported by pillars. These buildings, partly underground, are built up with

Hypostyle chamber at Torre d'en Galmés

Navetas (illustrated below and on page 125)

So named in 1818 by Juán Ramis y Ramis, the first Spanish writer on Menorcan prehistory, the *naveta* is a stone-built

large stones. They are roofed quite haphazardly with huge stones lying across the stone pillars, which are always much wider at the top than at the bottom.

Hypostyle chambers can be seen on Walks 2, 5, 7, 8, 13 (where one is still in use as an animal shed) and 15, as well as Picnics 5 and 13.

burial chamber which resembles an upside-down boat. Hence its name, from the Latin word for boat *(navis)*. The *naveta* was always built some distance from the village. Two walks visit *navetas*: 8 and 22.

Left: standing stone at Talatí de Dalt; above: naveta at Rafal Rubí

● Picnicking

Menorca abounds in quiet, shady, isolated, scenic spots perfect for picnicking. All the car tours and walks in this book indicate several such ideal places. Unfortunately, many of them are only accessible on foot and are not very close to bus stops.

There are 22 picnic suggestions on the following pages. All are indicated on the touring map by the symbol *P*. However, as many of the picnics lie along or near the route of walks, you can pinpoint their location on the appropriate large-scale *walking* map, where you will also find the symbol *P*.

All the information you need to get to these picnics is given below; 🚌: how to get there by bus; 🚗: where to park your car. Please glance over the comments before you start off on your picnic: if some walking is involved, remember to wear sensible shoes and to take a sunhat (○ = picnic in full sun.) Take a plastic groundsheet as well, in case the ground is damp or prickly.

1 ERMITA DE SANT JOAN (Car tours 1 and 2, Walk 3; town plan pages 36-37 and map on reverse of touring map; photograph page 45)

🚌 to Mahón. Follow Shorter walk 3, allowing about 40min on foot.
🚗 From the roundabout at the junction of the Me-3 and Me-7 above the port, head south on the dual carriageway. Turn right after 50m, then immediately left on a minor road. Park at the church (0.8km/0.5mi). **No walking.**

2 CALA DE SANT ESTEVE ('ST STEPHEN'S CREEK'; Car tour 1, Walk 4; map on reverse of touring map; nearby photograph page 100)

🚌 to Es Castell; then follow notes for motorists below. **40min on foot.**
🚗 Drive from Mahón past Es Castell. Keep straight on at the Sol del Este/Sant Lluís crossroads, and turn right just short of the army base along a narrow road. Follow the road round the *cala* and park at the end. Climb up beside an old tower to gain access to the coast, and picnic anywhere you like. Allow up to **10min on foot.** You will find some shade at the Torre d'en Penjat. (See also Picnic 17; it is close by.)

3 ES GRAU (Car tours 1 and 2, Walk 2; map page 41; photograph of a similar setting page 42, top right)

🚌 from Mahón to Es Grau; then see notes for motorists below.
🚗 Drive along the Fornells road (Me-7) from Mahón and in 0.8km/0.5mi take the first road on the right for Es Grau. Park by the beach. There are two pine-shaded picnic places near this magnificent beach. One is among the trees which border the beach itself. For the second, allow up to **20min on foot:** walk to the end of the beach and follow a path up the cliff. Turn left at the top and descend a track to a little valley, where you will find an open space among trees. For a short walk, follow the track round to the right, up out of the valley, and turn right at the top, by a wall. Then follow the track back towards Es Grau (seen ahead). Turn right at a junction, go down into a valley, then climb steeply, to regain your outgoing route. Keep straight on, back to the beach.

Climbing the old Roman road to Santa Agueda (Picnic 8; Car tour 2). See also notes in the panel on page 65.

4 CALA MORELL (Car tour 2, Walk 23; map page 130; photos on pages 12, 131)

🚗 to Cala Morell; park in the car park on the right. The rocks may be too crowded, but the area around the caves, described in Walk 23 (page 132), should be quieter; up to **5min** on foot.

5 TALATI DE DALT (Car tour 2, Walks 7 and 8; map on reverse of touring map; photographs on pages 1, 13, 60-61)

🚗 Leave Mahón along the Me-1. In 4km turn south along a metalled lane, signposted Talatí de Dalt, for 0.5km. Park in the parking area. The notes for Walks 7 and 8 tell you more about the site, usually quiet enough for a peaceful picnic. An entrance fee is payable.

6 CALA MESQUIDA (Car tour 1; map on reverse of touring map) ○

🚗 Park at the rear of the splendid, usually quiet, Cala Mesquida. Picnic on the beach, or explore the cliffs.

7 CALA PRESILI (Car tour 1; touring map) ○

🚗 Drive from Mahón towards Fornells along the Me-7, and turn right in 9km along a road signposted 'Fo. de Favaritx'. Park at the end of the road, by the entrance to the lighthouse (at the KM2 marker). Allowing **20min on foot**, walk back 0.7km/0.5mi to the small 100m-marker with the number 3. Turn left here along a rocky track, and in seven minutes turn left at junction. Five minutes later you reach the small beach. (You can take a much longer walk here, following the waymarked Camí de Cavalls described on page 100.)

8 SANTA AGUEDA (Car tour 2; touring map; photograph above)

🚗 Turn north off the Me-1 some 3km northwest of Ferreries, towards the hill of Santa Agueda, and in 3km park beside the former village school. To the right of the school a gate gives onto a path, a Roman road, still partly paved. In **5min** you reach a quiet shady spot with stones to sit on; **30min** brings you to the top of the hill, where the Romans had a fortress and a Moorish king had his summer palace. Here too the Moors made their last stand against King Alfonso in 1287.

9 SA ROCA DE S'INDIO (Car tour 1; touring map) 🛆○

🚗 Park 2km south of Es Mercadal on the Me-1. The site is named for the rock opposite, which viewed from here resembles a Red Indian chief. Benches, but no shade. Not worth going out of your way, but the only place to stop to eat off the main road between Mahón and Ciutadella. **No walking.**

10 CALA MITJANA (Car tour 2, Walk 16; map pages 96-97; photograph page 29)

🚌 to Cala Galdana. Follow the directions for Short walk 16. Allow up to **40min** on foot.
🚗 Drive towards Cala Santa Galdana. Turn left through a gateway signposted 'Cala Mitjana' 0.5km short of the roundabout at the entrance to Cala Galdana and drive along a farm track to the beach. **No walking.**

11 CALA MACARELLA (Car tour 2, Walks 17-19; map pages 96-97; cover photograph)

🚌 to Cala Santa Galdana, then follow notes for motorists below and allow **40min on foot**.

🚗 Drive to Cala Santa Galdana. On reaching the roundabout outside the town, take the second exit to the bay; there is a large car park on the right. Now allow **40min on foot**. Follow the first section of Walk 18 from Cala Santa Caldana to Cala Macarella, using the notes on pages 105-106. Cafetería Susy is open from late April to October.

12 CALA PREGONDA (Car tours 1 and 2; touring map) ○

🚗 Drive to the roundabout on the outskirts of Es Mercadal on the Alaior side. Follow the ring road (initially towards 'Fornells'). Go straight ahead at the next roundabout and over a crossroads, but at the third roundabout take the second exit for 'Platges Costa Nord' along the Camí de Tramuntana. Turn right at the T-junction and leave the town along a narrow country road. Ignore the first road on the right, but after 6.5km turn sharply right for Binimel·là. After 0.5km turn left along a wide dirt road. In 1km pass through a narrow gateway, and after a short distance turn left down a track to the beach. Park here, being careful to avoid soft sand. Now allow **25min on foot**. Walk left along the beach. Leave it before you get to the end, forking diagonally left on a path between low bushes. Make for a wall ahead, climb over and follow a wide track across the next beach, and to another wall. Go through a gap in the corner, and follow the path diagonally ahead towards white cliffs. Cross some sand dunes, another beach, more dunes, and climb towards one more wall. Make for the last concrete pole supporting power lines, and go through an iron gate. Turn right on a wide track above the beach, finally descending along a narrow path to the beach.

13 TORRE TRENCADA (Car tour 2, Walks 17 and 22; map pages 96-97) 🏠

🚗 Coming from Ciutadella on the Me-1, turn right shortly before the KM39 marker along a country lane signposted 'Torre Trencada'. Turn left at the T-junction, and after 2km park in a small car park. Follow the signposted path to the site of the prehistoric settlement of Torre Trencada (**8min on foot**), with its megalithic picnic table set beneath ancient olive trees in the middle of a prehistoric village.

14 CALO D'ES RAFALET (Car tour 1, Walk 12; map page 80)

🚌 to S'Algar; then see notes for motorists below.

🚗 Drive to S'Algar. Turn right as you enter the resort, and park in the car park on your right. Allow **40min on foot**. Walk down to the seafront and turn left. At the end of the seafront, walk past a wall, turn left, and walk uphill beside it. Continue with the sea to your right, up to the top of the hill. Use the stile to climb over the wall here, turn left and walk parallel with the creek, to the end of a long field. Turn right, and go downhill to a gap in the wall. Cross another field to leave through the gap at the wall's end. Turn right along a track, and in 20m/yds turn right again. As the track turns left, look for a gap in the wall on your right after 20m/yds (waymarked with a red arrow on a tree). Turn right and follow the path along a dried-up river bed to the end, where you will find a shady picnic area. Follow the path on to a tiny sandy beach and lovely little cove.

15 CALES COVES from Cala'n Porter (Car tour 1; touring map)

🚌 to Cala'n Porter. From the bus stop allow **35min on foot**. Bear left and walk uphill along the main street to the cliff edge, following signs for the

'Cova d'en Xoroi'. Now refer to notes for motorists below.

🚗 Drive to Cala'n Porter. Do not take the road on the right down to the beach, but go straight through the town to the cliff edge. Park where convenient and allow about **15min on foot**. Turn left along the cliff edge, and follow any of the several paths parallel with the sea which is rarely more than 12m/yds away. In ten minutes you will be looking over the end of the creek. The path turns left here, parallel now with the *cala*. In about five minutes you will come to a place where you have a good view of the prehistoric caves in the cliffs opposite. Behind you the pine wood offers several open shady areas just right for picnicking on a hot day.

16 CALES COVES from Son Vitamina (Car tour 1; touring map) ○

🚌 Take the Cala'n Porter bus from Mahón and alight at the Son Vitamina bus stop. Walk up the side road for 150m/yds to a roundabout; then see notes for motorists below.

🚗 Leave the Maó/Cala'n Porter road at the Cales Coves sign. Drive up the side road for 150m/yds to a roundabout. Just beyond it is a parking area. Walk back to the roundabout, bear left, then turn left down a track signposted 'Cales Coves' and allow **30min on foot**. Walk down the track on your right, to arrive at a picturesque creek in whose cliffs are many prehistoric caves.

17 FORT ST PHILIP (Car tour 1, Walk 4; map on reverse of touring map; photograph page 49) ○

🚌 to Es Castell and **25min on foot**. Walk southeast beside the main road as far as the Sol del Este crossroads. Turn left and walk towards the sea. Now refer to notes for motorists below.

🚗 Drive from Mahón past Es Castell as far as the Sol del Este crossroads. Turn left and park just before the road bends left. Now allow **5min on foot**. Follow the road round to the left and on for 100m/yds, as far as the Cafetería Sol del Este. Turn right beyond it down an unnamed passage, to the coastal path at the end. Turn right to reach a wall with a stile, which gives you access to the site of Fort St Philip and a superb picnic spot where you can watch the cruise liners in the harbour. There are exceptional views of the harbour mouth, Sa Mola and the Illa del Llatzeret. Explore the remains of Fort St Philip as far as the *zona militar*. (Note that Picnic 2 is nearby, on the south side of St Stephen's Creek.)

18 SON BOU (Car tour 2, Walk 11; map pages 74-75; photographs pages 75 and 76) 🏕

🚌 to Son Bou. Walk down the road towards the beach; then see notes for motorists below. **2min on foot**.

🚗 to Son Bou. Park in the car park beside the beach, and leave by the entrance you drove in. As you turn towards the beach you will see in front of you a well-appointed pine-shaded picnic site with benches and tables. **No walking.**

19 CALA DE ALGAIARENS (Walk 23; map page 130)

🚗 Head from Ciutadella to Cala Morell, but when the Cala Morell road turns left, keep straight on for 3km/2mi to the turn-off left. The beach and car park lie through private property, so expect to pay a parking fee (well worth it). There are shaded picnic tables, toilets (of a sort), and a wonderful beach. **No walking** or follow the Camí de Cavalls (see page 100) as far as you like.

20 CALA SON SAURA (Walk 18; map page 103 and touring map)

🚗 Leave Ciutadella on the Cala'n Turqueta road, but fork right after 3km/2mi on a good road. In 3km/2mi you will pass the 'poblat', or prehistoric village, of Son Catlar and in a further 2km/1.3mi arrive at the

FLOWERS, BIRDS AND TORTOISES

Menorca is wonderfully rich in wild flowers and birds. Although having the characteristic brown appearance of Mediterranean countries during July and August, for most of the year the island's ample rainfall gives it a rich green colouring, splashed with the vivid hues of its multitude of flowers. Left to itself, I suppose that the mastic bush, *Pistacia lentiscus*, would soon take over the whole island. You will see it everywhere — growing out of walls and blocking footpaths you want to use, covering *talayots*, trapped behind stone walls in the middle of every field. There are many other bushes and shrubs to be found, including myrtle and juniper, wild olive and fig, but very few trees. The pine is the only common real tree, especially *Pinus halepensis*, the Aleppo pine, although *Pinus pinea*, the umbrella pine, is also to be found. Mercifully the bushes are more or less contained, allowing such a variety of wayside flowers to flourish as to excite wonder and envy in the English visitor. Over a thousand species of plant have been identified on the island, and what is in flower will depend on the month of your visit. In early summer the gardener whose pride is in his gladioli will certainly see *Gladiolus communis*, its wild ancestor. Widespread and spectacular is *Hedysarum coronarium*, with red lupin-like flowers. In the same season you will see everywhere asphodel with white flowers raised high on long stems above yucca-like leaves. The pasture fields are filled with variegated thistles and walls festooned with pink *Convolvulus althaeoides*, wild roses and *Cistus*. Common 'weeds' of the verges are the herb fennel, whose feathery leaves smell of aniseed, and vivid red poppies. October sees the autumn crocus whose delight is to push through the bare earth of the tracks you walk along.

In high summer the flowers are dead, but the withered seed heads of this multitude of plants feed an equal abundance of birds at this time, none more prolific than the goldfinch, while in spring and early summer the song of birds is unending wherever you walk.

The national bird is the red kite. It is unmistakable, and rarely will you complete a walk without one slowly circling above your head. It is a very large bird, with wings ending in 'fingers' spread wide. From below, silhouetted, the large white patches under its wings and its deeply forked tail make it easy to identify. Seen from above when it swoops into a valley, the sun blazing down upon it, it is magnificent.

Another large bird which behaves in a similar way, but is much less common, is the booted eagle. Its tail is wedge-shaped however, and it has a broad white band across the top of its wings — just the opposite of the kite, so that you need to be above it to be sure of identifying it.

Most large white birds circling round pretending to be hawks will be herring gulls. You will always know when a fishing boat is coming in by the cloud of herring gulls above it.

However, if a large white bird looks like a kite, but with the white and black bands beneath its wings reversed, you are having the good fortune to see an Egyptian vulture.

All the little birds you see seem to have black heads and pale bellies. This is because it is a characteristic of four very common species: blackcap, Sardinian warbler, stonechat and pied flycatcher. The stonechat is probably the easiest of the four to pick out. His back is black as well as his head, and he has a red breast, so that he looks a bit like a black robin. He loves to perch on some spike rising above the bush, and is not too timid, so that he will often sit there 'chatting' while you get a good look at him.

Crows are rare, but one that you will see is the raven, usually alone. The following are also quite common: short-toed and crested larks, alpine swifts (there are ordinary swifts too), grey and purple herons, corn buntings, kestrels, linnets, crag martins, house martins, swallows, tawny pipits (like wagtails, only brown), spotted flycatchers, red-legged partridges, house sparrows, nightingales, whinchats, rock pigeons, turtle doves.

There are several waders and ducks that you may see in the bays and lagoons, especially at S'Albufera. Cormorants are common. I once saw one at Santandría standing for ages, hanging its wings out to dry, surrounded by small children who thought it was a penguin.

I have left the best two until last. One is quite a large bird, glorious pink in colour, with a splendid crest and wings that look like a piano keyboard when it flies past. It is the hoopoe. I have met them on many of my walks, usually in pairs, and always with the same thrill of excitement. The other is the bee-eater, described on page 44.

As for the rest of the fauna, there are snails and lizards everywhere, especially in the drystone walls. Black beetles, butterflies and bees abound. But the really exotic creature which will delight your children is the tortoise, often seen on woodland paths.

gateway to the Torre Saura Vell estate, where you will pay a parking fee. Drive 2km along a fairly good farm track to a car park. There are shaded picnic tables beyond the car park as well as a fabulous beach. **No walking.**

21 SON CATLAR (touring map)

🚗 Leave Ciutadella on the Cala'n Turqueta road, but fork right after 3km/2mi on a good road In 3km/2mi you will come to the 'poblat', or prehistoric village, of Son Catlar. It is maintained by the same group of archaeological enthusiasts that looks after the site of Picnic 5. There is a large car park. The prehistoric village is completely enclosed by its original wall, all 870m/yds of it. There is plenty of shade. Expect to pay an entrance fee. **Very short walk.**

22 TORRE LLAFUDA (Car tour 2; touring map)

🚗 Shortly after the km37 marker on the Me-1 there is a notice board beside the lane leading to Son Sintes farm announcing Torre Llafuda. Turn here and drive along the lane for 0.8km/0.5mi. There is a car park and a small but very pretty *poblat* or prehistoric village with *talayot, taulas* and burial caves. It is usually quiet and there is plenty of shade. **No walking.**

☀ Touring

There are many car hire firms on Menorca, or you can reserve a car via your travel agent or holiday company at home. Charges can vary considerably, so shop around. The cheapest deal does not necessarily mean the worst car. Be certain to ask for and get 'Collision Damage Waiver', otherwise you will be liable for any repair bill for the car that you incur. On which topic, a word of warning. If you are only used to right-hand drive cars and driving on the left, then collecting your totally unfamiliar car at the airport, after dark (when you forgot you had to drive and so had a few drinks on the flight), can be unnerving.

Always check your vehicle in advance and point out any existing dents, scratches etc. Ask for all the conditions and insurance cover in writing, in English. Check to make sure you have a sound spare tyre and all the necessary tools. Be sure to get the office and the after-hours telephone numbers of the hire firm and carry them with you. If you are not 100% happy with the car, don't take it. Finally, if you pay by credit card, make a note of exactly what you are signing for.

The two car tours will take you to the majority of the notable places on the island (indicated with a ★ in the touring notes and on the touring map). The touring notes are quite brief. I concentrate instead on the 'logistics' of touring and the possibilities for nearby **countryside picnics** and **walks**. (Usually further historical notes can be found in the text with the relevant walk or in the boxed panels listed on page 4.)

The large fold-out touring map is designed to be held out opposite the touring notes and contains all the information you will need outside the towns. Town plans of Mahón and Ciutadella, showing exits for motorists, are on pages 36-37 and 114-115 respectively. **Remember to allow plenty of time for visits.** The times given in the tours are actual driving times, and no allowance has been made for time spent sightseeing. The distances quoted in the notes are *cumulative kilometres* from the departure point. A key **to the symbols** used in the touring notes is on the touring map.

All motorists should read the Country code on page 10 and go quietly in the countryside.

Once a fishing village, Fornells (Car tour 1) is now the most chic resort on the island, visited by Spanish royalty.

Car tour 1: EASTERN MENORCA

Mahón/Maó • Favaritx • Arenal d'en Castell • Fornells •
Es Mercadal • Monte Toro • Alaior • Torralba • Cala'n
Porter • (Cales Coves) • Sant Climent • Binibeca Vell • Sant
Lluís • Es Castell • Mahón/Maó

129km/81mi; about 4 hours' driving

On route: Picnics (see pages 14-19) 1, 2, 3, 6, 7, 9, 12, 14, 15, 16, 17; Walks
1, 2, 3, 4, 5, 6, 7, 8, 9, 10, 12

*The roads are generally good and adequately wide, although occasionally bumpy.
There are petrol stations in Mahón (Maó), on the Me-7 two kilometres before the
Arenal turn-off, and in Alaior.* **Important:** *although the driving time is only four
hours, allow an entire day if you want to visit all the tourist attractions.*

A modern highway, the Me-1, runs across Menorca connecting the capital Mahón (Maó) with the second largest
town and former capital, Ciutadella. On it lie the three next
largest towns of the island — Alaior, Es Mercadal and Ferreries.
Just outside Mahón on this road there is a large roundabout,
which has been taken as the nominal start and finish of this tour,
although being circular it can be joined and left wherever is
convenient.

Coming from **Mahón★** (✝ 🏔 ▲ ✕ 📷 ☎ M; Walks 1, 3, 5-7;
notes page 33), turn right at the roundabout and follow the dual
carriageway downhill towards the port. At the bottom of the hill
turn left in the direction of Fornells along the Me-7 (a right turn
leads to Cala Mesquida; Picnic 6). This is the beginning of the
Camí d'en Kane (Kane's Road), built early in the 18th century
by the first British lieutenant-governor of Menorca, Sir Richard
Kane, to link Ciutadella in the north with Port Mahón, replacing
the earlier road built by the Romans. You will see a memorial to
him on your right soon after the start of the road. This first stretch
necessitated the draining of marshes, resulting in the creation of
the rich agricultural land on your left. The nearby Camí de Sant
Joan would take you to the setting for Picnic 1 and Walk 3.

Almost at once pass the Me-5 on the right to Es Grau★, a
tiny resort with a large beach (Picnic 3, Walk 2). Soon the Camí
d'en Kane bears away to the left. However you keep straight on
along the Me-7, following signs for Fornells. The road continues
in a northwesterly direction through a beautiful countryside of
lightly-wooded low hills. Some 2.8km beyond the Camí d'en
Kane turning, ignore another turn-off on the left (it leads to Walk
9c, but was closed to motorised traffic at time of writing, so use
the notes on page 66 if you are approaching Walk 9). Continue
towards Fornells for another kilometre, when you will pass on
your right a little church, the Ermita de Fátima.

Another road now goes to the right. It is signposted 'F(ar)o
(lighthouse) de Favaritx'. Turn along here. At first the road is
very straight as it crosses flat terrain, passing the estate of

Capifort, before winding between low green hills, to end at the lighthouse at **Cape Favaritx** (17.5km). There is car parking here and, 0.7km back along the road, a track on the left brings you in 12 minutes' walking to the beach of Cala Presili (Picnic 7). Perhaps you will return another day and try a hike along the Camí de Cavalls (see page 100) which runs both west and south from the lighthouse.

Returning to the Me-7, turn right to drive through increasingly wooded scenery. In 6.5km you pass a picnic area on the

Walk 6 passes this fortified farmhouse at Binissaida (see also pages 128-129).

left, just before a roundabout. Three resorts lie at the end of the road to the right: Arenal d'en Castell, Na Macaret and Puerto Addaia. Arenal probably has the most to offer you, although Puerto Addaia can provide a boat trip along a charming *cala*, the third longest in Menorca. All three are well signposted: turn right on the Me-9 and, when you come to a crossroads, go left for Arenal, straight on for Na Macaret, or right for Addaia. The long, curved beach at **Arenal d'en Castell** (36km ⌂⌂▲✕) is one of the best on the island (*arenal* means 'sandy beach'). The small seaside village of Na Macaret (▲✕) is one of the oldest holiday resorts on Menorca. Puerto Addaia (▲✕) overlooks the harbour. When in the mid-18th century John Armstrong wrote the first English guidebook to Menorca, he described Addaia as the most exquisite place on the island.

Again return to the Me-7, turn right and follow signs for Fornells. In 3km you will pass the turn-off right for Son Parc★ (▲✕ and Menorca's only golf course). After 6.5km you will reach another roundabout at the junction with the Me-15. Turn right. For 4km the road runs beside the second largest *cala* on Menorca. Remote from Ciutadella and Mahón, it was once a favourite anchorage of Mediterranean pirates. As a result no Menorcans would live there. In 1591 the governor decided that the time had come to do something about the pirates, and a start was made on fortifying the entrance to the harbour. The ruins of that fortress will be seen if you walk towards the harbour mouth. Under its protection the lovely fishing village of **Fornells**★ (51km ⬥▲✕📷; photograph pages 20-21) grew up. You can see on the Isla Sarganta in the bay a tower built by the British to provide crossfire and, on the headland overlooking the village and harbour entrance, a second tower.

Drive back beside the *cala* towards the roundabout and, just short of it, turn right on a country lane. After 2km you pass a wide road off right to Cala Tirant and 2km further on come to another road on your right (Cf-3), where I recommend a detour. It leads to the lighthouse on Cap de Cavalleria. Some 4km along this road, the little eco-museum is worth a visit. It is a further 3km from the museum to the lighthouse. After the detour, return to this junction and turn right to continue. After 2km you will pass on your right a wide dirt road. It leads to the beach of Binimel-là (the turn-off for Picnic 12). In 0.5km turn sharp left for Es Mercadal; you will pass one tarmac road on the left en route.

When you reach **Es Mercadal** (66km ⬥▲ ✕M) turn left to join the ring road. Take the second exit at the first roundabout and the last exit at the next, signposted '**Monte Toro**'. A short, steep, winding drive will take you to the summit★ of the moun-

Windmill housing the ethnological museum at Sant Lluís (Walk 12), date palm in Mahón's Parc Rochina, and shrine in a cave at Fornells

tain (69km ✝✕☏M; photographs page 71). At 358m/1175ft, this is the highest point on Menorca, from where the whole of the island can be seen. It is also the high point of Walk 10. Its name probably dates back to the time of the Moorish occupation, deriving from the Arabic word *tor* meaning 'mountain'. However the fact that *toro* means 'bull' in Spanish has caused a curious legend to arise. It is claimed that the bull in question hewed with its horns a statue of the Virgin Mary out of rock, and that the name of the mountain commemorates this miracle.

Return to Es Mercadal and turn left at the roundabout. Turn left at the next roundabout onto the Me-1 towards Mahón. Shortly after leaving the town you will pass the electricity substation on the right, and then at the top of the hill you will find on the left a picnic site, **Sa Roca de S'Indío** (⛩; Pic nic 9). The rock opposite bears an uncanny resemblance to a Hollywood Red Indian chief.

Approaching **Alaior** (80km ✝✕⛽M), ignore the bypass and bear left to drive through the town. Just before the end of the town, turn right along a road signposted 'Cala En Porter'. After 3km you will arrive at the important megalithic site of **Torralba d'en Salort★** (83km ∏). You will find more about Alaior in the notes for Walk 10, and about Torralba in those for Walk 8. The road bends to your right now, and passes close to two more important archaeological sites (∏), Torrellisa and So na Caçana, before reaching a T-junction with the Me-12 in 3.5km.

Turn right at this junction and you will shortly arrive at **Cala'n Porter** (91.5km ⌂⌂✕☏; Picnic 15). The fairly large holiday resort is built high above a fine beach. Set in the cliff at the end of the *cala* is the **Cave of Xoroi★**, a bar and nightclub built in a prehistoric cave dwelling. Leave Cala'n Porter by the road you came in on and, when you reach the Alaior junction, keep ahead towards Sant Climent and Mahón.

Recommended diversion. If you have time for a short walk (1h return), after 0.5km take the road on the right signposted 'Cales Coves'. Park near the roundabout (94.5km ▄▲✕) and walk down the rough track which ends at the head of one of the prettiest of all the *calas* and the impressive troglodytic site of Cales Coves★ (🚻🎦; Picnic 16).

The main tour makes straight for **Sant Climent** (98.5km ✕). At the end of the village turn right (by a restaurant). Notice the stone seats along the walls now. They were made to accommodate spectators of the trotting races, still popular in Menorca, which were formerly held along here. In 2.5km a road to the right leads to Cala Canutells, but unless you want to make this detour, keep straight on to **Binidalí**, and turn left when you reach the sea.

What follows is the nearest you can get on Menorca to a motorable coastal road. It is impossible to give detailed directions — there are so many tiny streets as you drive from one resort to the next. It scarcely matters which streets you go along, you cannot get lost. Just keep heading southeast, and as close to the coast as you can, following signs for Cap d'en Font, Binisafúa, Binibeca, Biniancola and Punta Prima — which you will pass, in that order, in the course of the next 10.5km. Do drive carefully and slowly through the resorts.

One that you should take time to explore is **Binibeca Vell★** (▲✕🎦). It was one of the first *urbanizaciones* and was designed to replicate a typical Menorcan fishing village (a curious conceit, since there is no such thing; you have already seen Menorca's only fishing village — Fornells — and it is nothing like this!). It has been described, not inaccurately, as the ideal setting for a folklore film. At the southeast tip of the island is **Punta Prima** (113km ▄▄▲✕). Here you turn left and head for Sant Lluís, some 5km distant. Halfway along, a road on the right leads to S'Algar and Picnic 14.

Sant Lluís★ (118.5 ✝▲✕M) is the starting point for Walk 12, where you can read more about its origins. On leaving, turn right towards Es Castell. As you pass the village of Trebalúger on the right, look for its prominent *talayot*. In 4km you will reach a crossroads near a cemetery. Until 1782 the road to the right led to the mighty Fort St Philip. Take it now to enjoy Picnic 2, or cross over for Picnic 17; otherwise turn left. You skirt to the left of **Es Castell** (123km ✝▄▄▲✕🎦M; described in the notes for Walk 4). Soon the road bends and dips to Cala Figuera. Turn right here, down to Mahón's harbour. Turn left and drive the full length of the harbour road. At the end, turn left at the roundabout, to climb to the next roundabout, where the tour began (129km).

Car tour 2: WESTERN MENORCA

Ciutadella • Cala Santa Galdana • Es Migjorn Gran • Sant Tomàs • Sant Jaume Mediterrani • Alaior • Mahón • Es Grau • Es Mercadal • Ferreries • Ciutadella

Distance: 150km/93mi; about 4 hours' driving

On route: Picnics (see pages 15-19) 1, 3, 4, 5, 8, 10, 11, 12, 13, 18, 22; Walks 2, 3, 7, 8, 10, 11, 13, 14, 15, 16, 17, 18, 19, 20, 21, 22, 23

The roads are generally adequately wide and well surfaced, although the road into Sant Jaume is bumpy. There are petrol stations in Ciutadella, Alaior, and just outside Es Mercadal. Note that there is a speed restriction on the Camí d'en Kane.
Important: *although the driving time is only four hours, allow a full day to visit all the tourist attractions.*

The ancient and fascinating city of Ciutadella has been chosen for the starting point of this tour, out of consideration for the many tourists settled in the resorts of the northwest of the island. Since the tour is circular it can, of course, be joined and left wherever is convenient.

Ciutadella★ (✝♠♦▲✕➤☞M) is the starting point for Walks 20-22; see notes page 113. Leave the town along the Camí de Maó, the beginning of the Me-1 highway to Mahón (Maó). After 4km look out for the **Naveta d'es Tudons★** (ㅍ) on your right. It is clearly signposted and there is ample parking. A visit to this monument, shown on page 125, is *de rigueur,* if only because of its claim to be the oldest roofed building in Europe.

Statue on the Me-1 at the entrance to Ciutadella

It is visited on Walk 22, where you can read more about it. At 5.3km, near the KM39 marker, turn right along a road signposted 'Torre Trencada'. Turn left at the T-junction, leave your car in the small parking area, and follow the path to the interesting prehistoric settlement visited on Walk 17 and Picnic 13. Then return to the Me-1 and turn right. In 2km, a lane on the right leads to yet another important prehistoric site, that of Torre Llafuda (⏢; Picnic 22). Just over 5km further along, you could take a detour up a minor road on the left, towards a hill with famous historical associations — Santa Agueda (264m/870ft; ⏢🕰). A short walk would take you to the settings for Picnic 8.

The main tour continues on the Me-1 towards Ferreries. In 2.5km a road on the right takes you to beautiful **Cala Santa Galdana★** (29km ⛰⛰🏠✕🕰; photograph page 98; Picnics 10 and 11, Walks 16-18; Shorter walk 19). When you reach the roundabout at the resort's entrance, take the last exit (signposted 'Hotel Gavilanes') and drive to the end, where you will have a panoramic view over the bay.

Return to the Me-1 and turn right towards Ferreries. In 0.5km you come to another junction on the right, at the entrance to Ferreries. Leave the Me-1 here, and drive along the Me-20 to **Es Migjorn Gran** (44.5km ⚲✕), a small town founded in 1763. Turn right on the far side of town, passing through a region rich in megalithic monuments (mostly not visible from the road). The road (Me-18) ends at a long beach of silver sand, at **Sant Tomàs★** (48.5km ⛰⛰🏠✕; Walks 11 and 13).

Return to Es Migjorn and keep straight ahead on the Me-18 towards Es Mercadal. In 3km turn right on the Me-16 towards Alaior and Mahón. In 4km you rejoin the Me-1. Turn right and, after 1km, take the next road on the right to **Sant Jaume Mediterrani★** (66.5km ⏢⛰⛰🏠✕). It has a long beach separated from lines of villas by a wide marsh. Turn left and drive to the far end of the resort — **Son Bou** (⚲), then turn right for the beach and car park (Picnic 18). Walk 11 starts here, and in the notes you can read more about the area, illustrated on pages 75 and 76.

Return to the T-junction, turn right and head back towards Alaior. After 5km turn right and, in 2km, keep left at a fork, to reach the largest of the cyclopean townships, **Torre d'en Galmés★** (74km ⏢; drawing page 13).

Drive back to the Son Bou/Alaior road and turn right. In 2.5km you will be back at the Me-1 just as it reaches **Alaior** (79km ⚲✕🛍M), the third largest town on Menorca. If you wish to see it, ignore the bypass and drive almost to the far side of the town, where you will see a road on the right signposted 'Cala En Porter'. If you drive a short distance along here, you should find room to park beside the road. Walks 8 and 10 start here, and the

Cala Mitjaneta, with Cala Mitjana beyond it (Walk 16 from Cala Santa Galdana)

notes for Walk 10 will tell you a little about the town. Otherwise carry on along the Me-1 as it bypasses the town, heading for Mahón. On the way you will pass four *navetas:* two on the right at L'Argentina, and two on the left at Rafal Rubí (all signposted and visible from the road). After 8km turn right on a minor road to the prehistoric site of **Talatí de Dalt★** (87.5km ⛪; Picnic 5; Walks 7 and 8; notes page 60; photographs on pages 1, 12-13 and 60-61).

Returning to the main road, continue *past* the industrial estate to a large roundabout in **Mahón** (the city is described on page 33). Turn left on the dual carriageway towards the port, and left again at the roundabout at the bottom of the hill.* In 0.7km take the Me-5 road on the right to **Es Grau★** (100km ▲✕; Picnic 3; Walk 2). Just as you reach this charming resort and its large and attractive beach, there is a turning to the left. Pull off the road here to admire the sea-water lagoon and nature reserve of S'Albufera, shown on page 42.

Go back to the Me-7 and turn right towards Fornells but, after 1.5km, turn left along the Camí d'en Kane. This road, described in Walk 3, affords pleasant driving through a rural landscape north of Alaior. Rejoin the Me-1 at a roundabout with the Es Mercadal bypass and follow signs for Ferreries and Ciutadella. Turning right here leads to Picnic 12. Both **Es Mercadal** (126km ⛽▲✕M) and Ferreries are market towns founded after the Reconquest. Just before the Me-1 (🚉) enters **Ferreries** (134km ⛽▲✕M), you pass a minor road on the right which is on the route of Walk 14; like Walk 15, it starts in Ferreries. After 150km you arrive back at Ciutadella, from where you have the easiest access to Walks 19 and 23, as well as Picnics 4 and 19-21.

*Circling this roundabout you can reach the lane to the Ermita de Sant Joan (Picnic 1 and Walk 3; photograph page 45); see Picnic 1 notes on page 14.

❀ Walking

The walks in this book cover a good cross-section of the island. I have tried to choose walks which take you to places of interest. In some cases that will be historical or archaeological. In others it will be a beautiful, remote beach or particularly appealing scenery. There are walks to suit every taste from short strolls to rambles over 20 kilometres long. For a selection of *very* short walks, see the picnic suggestions on pages 14 to 19.

To choose a walk that appeals to you, you might begin by looking at the touring map inside the back cover. Here you can see at a glance the overall terrain, the roads, and the location of the walks. Flipping through the book, you will see that there is at least one photograph for every walk. Having selected one or two potential excursions from the map and the photographs, turn to the relevant walk. At the top of the page you will find planning information.

What to take

These walks are not strenuous or dangerous. You are not likely to get lost nor, despite the feeling of isolation you will often have, are you ever likely to be very far away from the nearest town. Nonetheless it is worth giving some thought to what to take with you. **Footwear**, for example. I have always recommended well worn-in walking boots, for the protection they give to the ankles. But I have more recently experimented with walking/sports sandals and have been won over to them for summer walking. The only real problem occurs on a few occasions when you are ploughing through brambles, when your feet could be badly torn. Then boots are preferable. On those occasions you will also need long trousers. Beach sandals are *not* suitable for walking. Take a **bandage**, in case you do put your ankle out. In summer you will need a long-sleeved shirt for **protection against the sun**, and for the same reason a sunhat and long trousers. If the walk includes a beach, and many do, take a towel, swimwear and sun cream. Have **waterproof clothing** if it looks like rain, especially outside summer. You will need a **small rucksack** with a **first-aid kit** (include aspirin tablets), up-to-date **bus timetables**, and **water**. A **whistle** and **torch** are always advisable. Bird-lovers should try to have light-weight **binoculars**. For each walk in the book, the *minimum* equipment is listed. Use your good judgement to modify my equipment list according to the season!

Nuisances

While there are large **dogs** on the island, they are almost always tied up. You will come across a few small ones, not tied up, that continue to bark until they have seen you off their patch. In my experience, these have proved harmless but, if dogs worry you, buy an ultrasonic 'Dog Dazer' from www.sunflowerbooks. co.uk. The few **snakes** on the island are also harmless. The only real nuisance is the **mastic bush** *(Pistacia lentiscus)*, which flourishes on drystone walls and threatens to render impassable just about every walled-in track on the island. You should not have too much difficulty with any of the routes described in this book, but you *will* come across plenty of locked or blocked **gates**. *Do, please,* read all of the panel on page 42 about 'gates' before setting out on any of the country walks.

The walking notes

When you are on your walk, you will find that the text begins with an introduction and then quickly turns to a detailed description of the route. **Times** are given for reaching certain points in the walk. Note: I walk at an average speed of 4km/h (2.5mph), but far from consistently. *Do* compare your pace with mine on one of the short walks, before taking a long hike. *Remember, the time checks are from one point to the next and do not take into account any stops at all.* For an entire walk, it would be wise to increase the overall time *by about thirty percent.* The large-scale **maps** (all 1:40,000) have been specially annotated to show important landmarks; below is a key.

dual carriageway	— 200 — height (metres)	P picnic place (see pages 14-19)
main road	bus stop	
secondary road	car parking	cave.quarry
minor road	best views	threshing floor
unsurfaced road	picnic tables	building.fortified
cart track.wide path	church.chapel	watchtower
footpath.steps	cemetery	stadium. windmill
main walk/alternative	prehistoric site	page reference

Walk 1: A WALKABOUT TOUR OF MAHON

See town plan on pages 36-37

Distance: 5.3km/3.3mi; 2h10min

Grade: easy

Equipment: comfortable shoes of any sort, sunhat, raingear

How to get there and return: 🚌 or 🚗 to/from Mahón. There is an underground car park beneath the Plaça de S'Esplanada, but you may find it easier to park beside the harbour road. If you choose the latter, begin and end the walk at the 56min-point.

Shorter walk (2.5km/1.5mi; 1h30min; grade, equipment, access/return as above). Follow the main walk as far as the 16min-point, then turn right and walk beside the Carmen church. Walk in front of the church and cross the Plaça d'Espanya to the far right-hand corner, passing the fish market and the road leading down to the port. Turn right and pick up the main walk again at the 56min-point.

I suppose the people of Menorca and Malta will never agree whether the Grand Harbour at Valletta or Port Mahón is the finest harbour in the Mediterranean. That the Royal Navy settled in Valletta in the 19th and 20th centuries was due entirely to the decision of Admiral Lord Nelson. Cynics argue that his choice of Valletta was itself entirely due to the fact that Malta was considerably closer to the court of Naples where Lady Hamilton's husband was British ambassador. For a century before that decision was made, Port Mahón had been the home of the British Mediterranean fleet.

The walk begins in the **Plaça de S'Esplanada** (photograph page 39), close to the BUS STATION [1]. This is the largest and most attractive of a number of squares in Mahón, or Maó as it is usually called now. An 'esplanade' being the space between a citadel and the houses of a town, the name is apt, for on the west side the square is overlooked by BARRACKS [2] built during the British occupation. The square was their parade ground. In front of the barracks is the tall **Monument to the Civil War Dead** [3].

Stand with your back to the monument and face east. Walk to the street which leads away from the far right hand corner of the square. This is the CARRER DE SES MORERES. Since you will leave this street by turning right, perhaps you should cross over now and walk along the right-hand side. You can come back on the other side at the end of your tour, but crossing now will give you the opportunity to inspect the bust of Dr Orfila outside no 13, which was his birthplace. Mateu J Orfila (1787-1853) became Professor of Chemistry in the Medical Faculty of the University of Paris, and began the systematic study of poisons. He is regarded as the father of forensic medicine. This street is dedicated to him.

Ignore the street on your right called Cós de Gràcia, and walk

32

ABOUT THE CITY

The harbour at Mahón is three and a half miles in length, the longest and deepest of a number of fine harbours on the island. Although the harbourage here is excellent, being bordered by high cliffs it is somewhat inaccessible. However there was one place where a small cove cut into the cliff, and a path ran down to the sea. At the top of the cliff overlooking this cove a fortified village was built in ancient times.

View across Mahón harbour to the naval station and the city's three great churches

One of the first people on record to have anchored his ships here was a Carthaginian general in 206BC. His name was Mago, brother of the famous Hannibal. When the Romans named the village Municipium Flavianum Magontanum, they may have been naming it after him. Later it was to give its name to mayonnaise! After the Romans, Vandals and Byzantines in turn occupied Mahón until the coming of the Moors, and in 902AD Menorca became part of the Emirate of Cordova. The Moors wanted a harbour nearer to Spain, and built their capital at Ciutadella, but it was here at Mahón that the Reconquest of Menorca began.

On 5th January 1287 King Alfonso III of Aragón sailed into the harbour with twenty ships and landed on the Isla del Rei ('the King's Island'. After defeating the Moors, Alfonso resettled the island with Catalans. At various times in the future more and more settlers came from that eastern province of Spain, so that the language of the island came to be a form of Catalan known as 'Menorquín'. (This has been strongly revived since the accession of King Juan Carlos, and most of the former Spanish street names have been replaced with Menorquín names.) On 1st September 1535 the Turkish naval commander Kheir ed-Din Barbarossa ('Redbeard') sailed under false colours into the harbour, determined to exact vengeance for the sack of Tunis by the Emperor Charles V. The Turkish siege threw up a 'Menorcan Benedict

Arnold'. His name was Jaime Scala, the town bailiff. He came to an arrangement with Barbarossa to open the town gates, on the condition that he and his friends were spared. The town was sacked, and Barbarossa sailed away with 800 captives. The following year Jaime Scala was put on trial and executed for treason.

In the next century Mahón grew to become the most important town on the island, and the governor Admiral Oquendo moved his residence here. It was during the 18th century that Mahón reached its eminence, when Menorca became part of the British Empire. Today, with a population of some 25,000, Mahón is the capital of the island and its main shopping centre. For refreshment there is no lack of bars, cafés and restaurants, although the same cannot be said of hotels.

the length of Ses Moreres until the crossroads. Here turn right. Mahón is built on a not inconsiderable hill above the harbour. The descent is in two stages. This is the first, along CARRER BASTIO and down the COSTA D'EN DEIA. Halfway along, the way bends to the left. Stop here, and look carefully at the building on your left, on the corner — the **Teatro Principal** [4]. It was built as an opera house in 1829 to the design of an Italian architect. The interior was exquisite. At the bottom of this steep hill is a pretty little square, the **Plaça Reial**, at the heart of a pedestrianised shopping area.

Cross over the square and continue in the same direction along S'ARRAVALETA and into another square, known as the **Plaça del Carmé**. This is dominated by the massive church opposite you, which was built in 1751 as the conventual church of the Carmelite Order of nuns. It is now known as the Carmen or **Carmé Church** [5]. Baroque in style, its west front is quite plain, although it appears to have once been more ornate. It is worth seeing inside (the side door is in the south wall; you will pass it later in the Shorter walk). When digging the foundations for this church, the workmen unearthed many coins and other objects from the Roman period.

Now that the nuns are no longer here, the cloisters and garden of the convent have been beautifully transformed into a shopping and cultural centre. Cross to the far side of the square and go up steps to enter it. In the basement is a supermarket; small shops and boutiques line the cloisters, and on the first floor are music and art schools. The central garden, **Sa Plaça** [6], is now a fine paved square, from where the architecture of the convent buildings can be appreciated.

Leave by the door diagonally opposite the one you came in by. Pass a museum [7] and, at the end of a short street, you will find yourself in the **Plaça Miranda**. Turn left and walk to the end of the square overlooking the harbour for one of the most beautiful views on the island. Below are the docks; opposite is the naval station.

Now retrace your steps and walk back across the square. Carry on to the traffic lights and yet another little square — the **Plaça del Príncep** (**16min**). Cross over to the far side, passing an attractive house on your left, and turn left into the CAMI D'ES CASTELL. Follow this street to its end, then turn left (referring for a short time to the map on the reverse of the touring map). Pass in front of a petrol station and turn left along Avinguda Fort de l'Eau. At the next roundabout (the one with the anchor) fork right and go down to the HARBOUR (**30min**). Turn left once more to follow the road back into town beside one of the Mediterranean's prettiest harbours. The gloomy island on your right, now an hotel, is the Isla del Rei, and the red-painted house on the headland to the right was once the home of the Commander-in-Chief of the British fleet, Admiral Lord Collingwood. When you reach the COMMERCIAL DOCK (recognisable by the enormous cruise liner that will almost certainly be moored there), climb the steps on your left up through **Parc Rochina** [8]. At the top is the **Plaça d'Espanya** (**56min**). Turn right until you are virtually facing the direction you have just come from and, passing the end of the PORTAL DEL MAR, go up the hill beside Parc Rochina into another square. This is the **Plaça de la Conquesta**. On your left is the statue of young Alfonso III himself. He was 18 years old at the time of the Reconquest. The statue was given to the city by the late General Franco. The young king's generosity in donating land both to his followers and to the religious orders of St Francis and St Clare earned for him the title 'the Liberal'. (His successor, Jaime II, thought him far too liberal, and reclaimed many of his gifts to the orders.)

The building on the left of the square is **St Mary's Church**

Parc Rochina

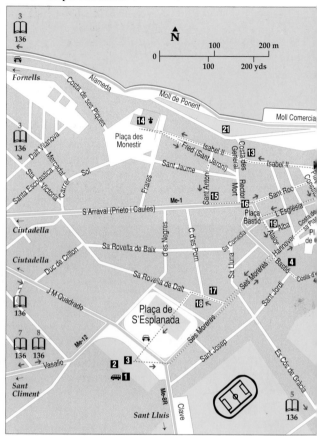

[9] (Santa María), and facing you is the **Casa Mercadel** [10]. Once the home of one of Mahón's noble families, it was built in 1761 on the foundations of the ancient castle, some of which is incorporated into the interior. This part of the town contains the oldest surviving buildings, and is on the site of the original town, within the medieval walls. The Casa Mercadel is now the Casa de Cultura. It contains a public library, an art gallery, and the town's archives. Turn right in front of the library, and go to the end of CARRER D'ALFONS III, beneath the **Pont d'Es Castell** arch [11]; here you have another enchanting view of the harbour.

Turn round now, and walk back past the Casa Mercadel and along the narrow cobbled street named after Alfonso III into yet another square, the **Plaça de la Constitució**. On your right is the **Ajuntament** [12], the Town Hall. It was first built in 1613, but entirely transformed in 1788. This too is open for inspection. Go up the steps leading from Carrer d'Alfons III to the

entrance beneath the clock in the short wall. The clock is English, a gift from the first British lieutenant-governor, Sir Richard Kane. In the entrance hall are pictures of former governors, the Comte de Lannion and the amiable looking Count of Cifuentes, governor during the period of Spanish rule from 1781 to 1798. There are two inscribed stones of interest. One is the British coat-of-arms that was removed from Fort St Philip when it was destroyed. The other, scarcely decipherable, records the granting of municipal status to the town by the Romans. At the end of Alfons III turn right, walk past the police station and, at the end, turn left along CARRER D'ISABEL II. This was the street where the medieval royal palace, and later the British governor's palace, were located. Consequently, the Mahón aristocracy chose to build its homes here. The present houses date from the 18th century and are in a curious mixture of English and Mediterranean styles. The two most apparent debts to English architecture are the sash windows and the absence of balconies. Sash windows are virtually unknown outside the British Isles, except for here in Mahón.

To appreciate these buildings properly you must look upwards. The main state rooms are on the first floor, the *piso principal*, and many still contain fine furniture made by the first-rate Menorcan craftsmen of the 18th century from the pattern books of English cabinet-makers like Chippendale and Sheraton.

Halfway along the street are the **Headquarters of the Military Governor** [13]. This is where Alfonso III built his palace in the 13th century, and where the British governor built his in the 18th. At first it was of only one storey, and the style is clearly British colonial. The narrow, arched street beyond it which leads down to the harbour is the COSTA DES GENERAL (or Es Pont des General) and was built either by the Moors, or very soon after the Reconquest.

Having investigated the Costa des General, continue along Isabel II. Notice the plaques above numbers 58, 60 and 62, commemorating illustrious inhabitants who were born or lived there. At the end of Isabel II is the **Plaça des Monestir**, where the **Church of Sant Francesc** [14] faces you. Once the friary of the Order of St Francis, it is decorated in a most unusual style, a mixture of baroque and Romanesque. Don't be fooled by the doorway — it was built at the same time as the rest of the baroque façade (sometime in the 17th or 18th centuries). The architect made similar use of primitive features inside. You may find it more difficult to gain admission to this church than the others in Mahón, but if the opportunity presents itself, seize it. Then go through the middle chapel on the right into one of the most exciting ecclesiastical experiences in the town — the Chapel of the Immaculate Conception.

Spanish religious architecture is generally almost puritanically severe — even, as you have already seen, during the baroque era. However, there is one exception. In the 18th century one Spanish architect went overboard in his reaction against this tendency. His name was José Churriguera, and the style which he invented is called after him 'churrigueresque'. Not only did he use baroque decorative invention to excess, he crowned it by doing everything in brilliant white. (Cynics have dubbed the style, not inappropriately, 'wedding-cake architecture'.) The effect, in small doses, can be stunning, as here. Before leaving, notice the *trompe l'oeil* paintings at the top of the pillars beside the sanctuary.

Next to the church is the **Museum of Menorcan Antiquities** (closed on Mondays in the summer); I heartily recommend a visit — if only to see the cloisters in which it is housed! Leave the museum, cross over the square to return to the town centre along the CARRER FRED (also called Carrer de Sant Jeroni). Take the first turning on the right, which is CARRER DE SANT ANTONI. St Anthony Abad ('Abbot') became the patron saint of Menorca, for it was on his feast day, January 17th, that Alfonso defeated the Moors at Es Vergé. Cross over the Carrer de Sant Jaume and, at the end, you come to S'ARRAVAL (also called Prieto i Caules). On the left, at the corner, is the church *(ermita)* of Sant Antoni, built in classical style. It was restored in 1978 by the Sa Nostra savings bank, and is now the **Sala de Cultura** [15], where concerts and exhibitions are held regularly.

Turn left, and there before you is all that remains of the medieval walls, the **Sant Roc Gate** [16]. Pass through the gate, and walk through the middle of the ancient town along the

Plaça de S'Esplanada

CARRER DE SANT ROC. This road is the start of the Me-1 which crosses the island to Ciutadella. At the end of Sant Roc you re-enter the **Plaça de la Constitució**.

Facing you is **St Mary's Church** [9]. It is the main church of Mahón. The present building dates from the middle of the 18th century, but the first church here was begun in 1287, immediately after the Reconquest. Like the Carmen church, its baroque façade is severely plain, but inside it is very different. The magnificent decoration surrounding the main altar and the equally magnificent organ are noteworthy. This splendid instrument was built in Barcelona in 1809 by the Swiss organ builder Kyburz. In the town archives are letters from the bishop to Admiral Lord Collingwood arranging for its transportation and protection at the height of the Napoleonic Wars. It has 4 keyboards, 51 stops and 30,000 pipes. Recitals are given every weekday between 11.00am and 11.30am from June to October on this organ. By the south entrance are two tablets which commemorate the French governors of Menorca, Yacinthe-Cajetan, the Compte de Lannion, and the Marquis de Fremeur.

Turn right at the end of Sant Roc (or cross over the square if you have visited the church) and then turn right again into CARRER DE L'ESGLESIA (Church Street), to walk back up another of the ancient streets to the PLAÇA BASTIO beside the Sant Roc Gate. Turn left at the end, and walk along a delightful little passage, the CARRER D'ALAIOR, into HANNOVER STREET. Named after the British royal family when Menorca was part of the Empire, it is one of the principal shopping streets of Mahón. This is quite a steep hill *(costa)*, hence its Menorquín name COSTA DE SA PLAÇA. Turn left and go down the hill, and shortly you pass the square for which the street is named — the **Plaça de Colón**. Having once more arrived at St Mary's Church, this time turn right along a wide, pedestrianised street, the main shopping street of Mahón — CARRER NOU (New Street). Look out for the Casa de Cultura, an exhibition gallery.

At the end, turn right in the **Plaça Reial**, and begin the climb back up COSTA D'EN DEIA and on into CARRER BASTIO. At the junction turn left into Ses Moreres and this time walk on the far side of the street. Cross over Carrer Sa Lluna, but when you come to SA ROVELLADA DE DALT, turn right. You will shortly pass the TOURIST INFORMATION OFFICE [17] on your right, and then, on your left, a building with the word 'ATENEO' over the door. This is the **Science Museum** [18] and is worth a visit. The intellectual hub of the town, it houses both a library and a natural history museum, as well as providing a meeting-place.

From here, continue along the street and take the first turning on the left, back to the **Plaça de S'Esplanada** (**2h10min**).

Walk 2: SA TORRETA

Distance: 12.5km/7.8mi; 3h15min   **Grade**: moderate

Equipment: comfortable footwear, sunhat, raingear, swimwear, picnic, plenty of water, suncream, towel, binoculars

How to get there and return: 🚌 or 🚗 to/from Es Grau. By car take the Me-7 (Fornells road) from Mahón and in 0.75km turn right along the Es Grau road. Park beside the beach.

Shorter walk: Cala Sa Torreta (9.5km/6mi; 2h30min; grade, access and equipment as above). Follow the main walk to the 50min-point, then turn right with the Camí de Cavalls instead of left. Follow the track past one beach, across a headland, past a small cove and on to the beach of Cala Sa Torreta. To return, pick up the main walk at the 1h50min-point.

This walk has just about everything you could ask for. It crosses lovely and isolated countryside. It passes by both the largest habitat for water fowl on the island and one of the least-visited prehistoric *talayot* and *taula* sites, then carries on to a magnificent (but seaweedy!) beach backed by a shaded picnic spot … that also happens to be adjacent to a breeding ground for bee-eaters. Finally, for the most part it does this along well-surfaced, easily-followed tracks.

Begin by walking round the large SANDY BEACH of **Es Grau** (Picnic 3) to the cliffs at the far side. Climb the path up the cliff and cross the headland. At the top ignore the path which goes off to the right (your return route), and follow the wider path to the left as it curves round the end of a small valley. This path keeps turning to the left, soon entering a wooded area where you will find an OPEN SHADED SPOT just right for a picnic (another setting for Picnic 3; **20min**). In a little while you meet a junction. Ignore the path to the left, and follow the main path as it climbs round to the right. Shortly you will reach the top of your climb and come out of the trees to arrive at another junction. Ignore the path downhill to the left and in 80m/yds go through a gap in a wall. Ahead you will see Es Grau. Follow the path for about 350m/yds, ignoring any turnings to the right, and you will come

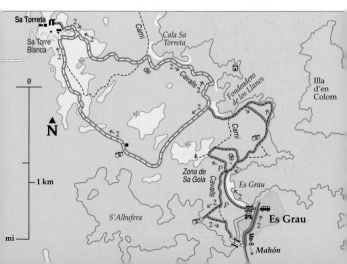

MENORCAN GATES

Look out for the aesthetically pleasing gates that still frequently stand at the entrance to farms and fields (the one in the photograph on page 91 is a good example). Made to a traditional Menorcan design from the twisted wood of wild olive trees, once they were universal, but lately farmers have been replacing them with sturdier iron ones like the one shown above. Alas, these prove harder to climb over … and perhaps this has not escaped the notice of the farmers!

Gates have attracted more correspondence from 'Landscapers' who use this book than any other subject. Let me try to clarify the matter. There are many references to gates and gateways in these walks, even across some public roads. They are mostly there to prevent cattle from straying. Farmers cannot afford to take the chance that people using the roads can be relied upon to close the gates securely behind them, so they will often padlock them (although not usually on public roads).

Top left: iron gate with a charming notice for walkers (Walk 9). Above: Cala Sa Torreta (top) is a pleasant place to picnic — nearby is a breeding ground for bee-eaters; S'Albufera, a salt-water lagoon (middle); the Fondeadero de los Llanes, with its pretty coves and watchtower (bottom)

So, depending on whether there is livestock in the vicinity, a gate may be open or closed. If the latter, it may be latched, secured with twine or padlocked. Hence you may be able to walk through the gate, need to open and secure it behind you, climb over it or climb over an adjacent wall. Very occasionally the latter may require a modicum of agility!

The situation can change from day to day, even from hour to hour. However, the farmer does not want the bother of getting out of his car to open and lock gates any more than you do, so please just remember that when a gate is locked, there is a good reason.

to another T-junction. Turn left here, fork left in 40m/yds, and head in the direction of the island known as Illa d'en Colom.

When you reach the cliffs, follow the path down to your left and walk along the edge of the cliffs. Eventually the path will fork. It does not matter which you choose, since they will shortly meet up, so I suggest you keep to the coastal path now and return by the other. Soon you will see below you an exquisite tiny beach, and at the end of the headland you will have a good view of an old watchtower and the lighthouse at Favaritx. Carry on round the edge of the cliff until, at the far side, you find yourself back on a clearly discernible path and join the other path you ignored at the fork. Follow the path down to sea level again and round the bay, past two small inlets and a sandy beach (**Fondeadero de los Llanes**, where you join the Camí de Cavalls), then up the slope on the far side. A tiny sandy path takes you through a gap in a wall and down to the left, where you join a track. *Note this junction for your return* (the pampas grass should help, and there should be a Camí de Cavalls marker post).

Turn left (**50min**) and follow the track southwest.* *(But for the Shorter walk, turn right here.)* After 200m/yds go through a gateway as the track takes you along a pleasant valley before bringing you within sight of the extensive salt-water lagoon of S'Albufera, home to a wide variety of water birds. The track now changes direction (**1h10min**), turning northwest and going through a gap in a wall by a stone shed, before it begins to climb more steeply. Go through another gap and climb up towards trees. After 15 minutes, walk between walls for a short stretch. Ahead you can see the farm of Sa Torre Blanca. It is your next port of call, but at present you are diverting into a field. At the end of the field you rejoin the track, and in a few metres/yards go through a gateway (**1h30min**). Turn left immediately and, as you head for the farm, you will see a *talayot* in front of you. When you reach the FARM OF SA TORRE BLANCA, go through the gate facing you and turn right. Follow the track beside the farm wall for 130m/yds, then turn left and enter the farmyard. Pass to the right of an old THRESHING FLOOR and, just before reaching the farm buildings, turn right through a wide gap in a wall. Take the path across the field, go through a similar gap, and turn left to the **prehistoric village of Sa Torreta**, complete with *talayot* and *taula* in its typical setting of standing stones within an over-grown walled enclosure. It is claimed that the *taula* here is one of the latest, 1000 years separating it from the earliest to be built.

*If you find this route blocked, turn *right* here (as for the Shorter walk) and do an out-and-back to Sa Torreta (see map). Go right at the Y-fork in front of the Torre Blanca farm and, with the threshing floor to your left, follow the notes above (from the old threshing floor, just after the 1h30min-point).

When you leave the site, retrace your steps to the threshing floor, go through a gateway in a wall, and ignore a further gateway on the left. The track descends through wooded country and opens out into a pretty valley, at the end of which you come to **Cala Sa Torreta** (**1h50min**). The way turns right to run along the back of a very beautiful and almost always deserted beach. Deserted, because it is probably the most seaweedy beach in Menorca. To your right pine trees provide a shaded picnic spot (photograph page 42). Beyond the wood, the small holes you may see in the sand bank are the nesting places of bee-eaters. If you are not an ornithologist, look for something the size of a pigeon and as colourful as a parrot.

By now you have rejoined the Camí de Cavalls. The track leads you next through trees. Leaving them, it swings left towards the sea and climbs to the right of a small building, running beside a wall to the next cove. Here it moves away from the wall and shortly turns right, away from the sea. In a few minutes it brings you across the headland to another delightful beach. In three or four minutes start to look for the tiny sandy path leading through the pampas grass on the left, which takes you back to the **Fondeadero de los Llanes** (**2h05min**). Go back through the gap in the wall and down to the beach. Round the beach and, at the far side, go through a gap in the rocks just at the water's edge. Follow the path as it circles the bay (ignoring the Camí de Cavalls heading up to the right). Beyond the last little inlet, the path climbs up the cliff. Fork right at the top and cross the headland; small cairns mark your way every few metres/yards. Once more pass behind the little beach, go through the gap in the wall, and follow the path uphill. At the top bear left; ignore two paths on the left, and the path on the right along which you came out. Head downhill towards the sea, with Es Grau clearly visible. At the bottom go straight over the crossing path and up a steepish climb. Ignore the right turn at the top, but follow the path ahead (Camí de Cavalls) until you regain the BEACH OF **Es Grau** (**2h45min**).

Do not round the beach, but continue in the same direction along the Camí de Cavalls and cross the end of the beach, to a gap between sand dunes. Here take a wide path which swings left through woodland. This is the **Zona de Sa Gola**, a 'Region of Special Natural Interest'. In three minutes, at a sign 'MIRADOR', follow a path on raised decking across a field towards **S'Albufera**, the lagoon. It takes you up a small hill to a platform, for perhaps the best view of the whole walk. On your return from the viewpoint, turn right where the decking forks. When you reach the main path/*Camí*, bear right. A track takes you across a footbridge and to the tarmac road. Turn left and in 250m/yds you will arrive back at the car park/bus stop at **Es Grau** (**3h15min**).

Walk 3: ES VERGE AND THE ERMITA DE SANT JOAN

See map on reverse of touring map; see also photographs pages 33, 35, 39

Distance: 10.5km/ 6.5mi; 2h25min

Grade: easy

Equipment: comfortable footwear, sunhat, suncream, raingear, picnic

How to get there and return: As Walk 1, page 32, but by 🚗 park either at the Plaça de S'Esplanada or at the western end of the harbour (the 15min-point in the main walk).

Shorter walk: Ermita de Sant Joan (4km/2.5mi; 1h10min; grade, equipment, access as above). Follow the main walk to the 40min-point, then skip to the 1h55min-point to end this stroll.

Photo: Ermita de Sant Joan

T his short and delightful walk is steeped in history. It takes you first along part of the Mahón waterfront and then through the fertile market gardens of Es Vergé, to the little Ermita de Sant Joan. From here you follow Kane's Dyke. Returning to the *ermita*, you make your way back to Mahón along a narrow lane of considerable antiquity, with splendid views over the plain.

Start out in **Mahón** by standing with your back towards the **Monument to the Civil War Dead** in the **Plaça de S'Esplanada** (see town plan on pages 36-37). Leave the square by the far left-hand corner and turn left into CARRER DE SA ROVELLADA DE DALT. Follow it round until you reach S'ARRAVAL. Cross over and continue ahead along CARRER DEL SOL, descending until you are in sight of St Francis' church and the Museum of Menorcan Antiquities. Bear left now and follow COSTA DE SES PIQUES downhill. Halfway down, turn right and go down steps to the port. The monument on your left was raised in 1785 by the people of Mahon in gratitude to the Count of Cifuentes (see page 37). Turn left and follow the road to the end of the harbour (**15min**). Take the road on the left signposted 'FORNELLS', not the one which goes across the end of the harbour. This is quite a busy road, and you should walk on the left-hand side of it. However, you will not be on it for long. It is the start of the main road which the first British lieutenant-governor of the island, Sir Richard Kane, had built to link Ciutadella with Mahón in the 18th century (the Menorcans know it as the 'CAMI D'EN KANE'). It runs parallel with the modern road (Me-1), about a kilometre to the north, as far as Es Mercadal, from where the Me-1 follows the line of Kane's road for the rest of the way. Before the British occupation, travel had been along the 'Old Road', the Camí Vell, first built by the Romans. It is significant that whereas the modern road goes to Mahón town, Kane built his road straight to the harbour. That was the only interest Britain had in Menorca

45

— a base for its Mediterranean fleet. Incidentally, Kane arranged for his road to be paid for in a very English way. He put a tax on alcohol.

In 200 metres/yards you come to a ROUNDABOUT. Turn left and walk up the hill for 60m/yds, then cross the ring road (RM) *carefully*. On the far side, walk ahead on asphalt for 40m/yds to a T-junction. Turn left here on a country lane, the Camí de Sant Joan (**30min**). You make your way through **Es Vergé**, between some of the most important market gardens on Menorca, which provide Mahón with its salad crops and vegetables. It is very peaceful down here, and the world of the tourist resorts seems far away indeed. It was here, at the head of the harbour, that eighteen year old Alfonso III met and defeated the Moorish army on 17th January 1287 and regained Menorca for Christendom. If you look over to your right, on the far side of the Fornells road, you will see a memorial which the people of Menorca raised to Sir Richard Kane in 1924.

After 650m/0.4mi the lane passes a little church on the left, the **Ermita de Sant Joan** (St John the Baptist; **40min**). This was clearly a place of communal importance in bygone days, with its stone seats around the little square. Now it has a neglected air, but young people at least have not deserted it completely, and it makes a wonderful place for a quiet picnic (Picnic 1). From here follow the road as it bends to the right and right again. *(But for the Shorter walk, skip to the 1h55min-point below.)* After 500m/ 0.4mi you cross a bridge and come to a T-junction. To continue the walk you will turn left, but before doing so you may wish to make a short detour to visit the **Kane Memorial** which you can see a short distance to the right along the Fornells road. For the rest of the outward part of the walk your way is beside a drainage ditch. Until the 18th century much of this plain was marshland. In order to build his new road across it, Kane had this ditch dug to drain the marsh, transforming it into rich agricultural land. The ditch abounds with vegetation and birds; keep beside it, ignoring all turnings on the right to farmhouses. Eventually you cross the ditch, and the road reverts to track.

Where the track divides, fork right (**1h**) along the CAMI D'ATZAGODARS and follow a walled-in track past bamboo. After heavy rain the track may be too muddy, forcing you to turn round here to continue the walk from the 1h25min-point, but most of the time you should be able to continue. You pass a pretty WHITE FARMHOUSE and carry on along a narrow metalled lane beside the dyke as far as a T-junction, where you turn left. Keep walking for a few more minutes — until houses, a gate, and a simple 'PROPRIEDAD PRIVADO, PROHIBIDO EL PASO' notice mark the end of the road.

Turn back here, enjoy the view, and retrace your steps past the white farm down to the MEADOW (**1h25min**). Turn left now and walk along the path by a high wall. Make your way back to the T-junction and turn right over the bridge, continuing as far as the **Ermita de Sant Joan** (**1h55min**). Turn right and walk in front of the church and between the trees. Take the CAMI DE DALT DE SANT JOAN on your left; it climbs up the hill behind a house. This is an ancient cart-road, which in the days before Kane drained the marsh was the only way from the farms of Es Vergé into Mahón. Where bedrock forms the surface, the deep ruts made by cartwheels over the centuries proclaim how much use this road has seen.

Soon you will come to where the modern harbour road (the RM dual carriageway ring road) cuts across the ancient one. Cross over with care and patience and go up a narrow path opposite. When the path turns right you will see that you are back on the ancient road. Most of the paving consists of small uneven cobbles, which was the normal Menorcan way of surfacing roads. Very occasionally, as in one section here (just before the track reaches the outskirts of the town), the paving is much more sophisticated and gives a clue to the origin of the road. Only the Romans surfaced roads with that much care before the 20th century, on Menorca or anywhere else (see panel on page 65).

The old road ends beside an INFANTS' SCHOOL (**2h10min**). Keep straight ahead, still on the CAMI DE DALT DE SANT JOAN, and cross over Carrer Cronista Riudavets. Continue in the same direction along CARRER SANTA VICTORIA, crossing **Plaça D'Eivissa**, Dalt Vilanova and Santa Escolàstica; then come to a T-junction. Turn right and follow CARRER SOL to its junction with S'Arraval (see town plan). Now, if you are in a hurry, cross over and follow Sa Rovellada de Dalt; in just over 200m/yds, it will bring you back to the Esplanade Square. Otherwise one more pleasure awaits you, especially if it is early evening. Turn left, and go along S'ARRAVAL as far as the **Sant Roc Gate**. Pass through the gate, go down the hill, cross the **Plaça de la Constitució**, and make your way along the narrow cobbled CARRER D'ALFONS III between the Ajuntament (Town Hall) and St Mary's Church. Cross the **Plaça de la Conquesta** and go on beneath the arch of the **Pont d'Es Castell**, to gaze out over Parc Rochina and the harbour. From here, walk back along ALFONS III to the **Plaça de la Constitució**, turn left and cross the square diagonally, to go up the hill of COSTA DE SA PLAÇA (Hannover) on the far left. Carry on into SES MORERES and back to the **Plaça de S'Esplanada** (**2h25min**).

Walk 4: FORT ST PHILIP AND MAHON HARBOUR

See map on reverse of touring map; see also photographs on pages 23, 33, 35, 39 and 53

Distance: 16km/10mi; 4h   **Grade:** easy

Equipment: comfortable footwear, sunhat, raingear, suncream, picnic (or have lunch in one of the restaurants en route), plenty of water

How to get there and return: 🚌 or 🚐 to/from Mahón. By car, park in the car park beneath the Esplanade Square. Alternatively take the ring road round Mahón, following signs for Es Castell. Park at the far side of the town, at the roundabout just west of Cala Figuera, and begin the walk at the 25min-point. At the end, turn to the start of the walk and follow the directions for the first 25 minutes to get back to your car.

Shorter walks

1   **Mahón and harbour** (4.5km/2.8mi; 1h; grade, equipment, access/ return as above). Follow the walk for 28min, then turn left and walk downhill past the petrol depot to the harbour road. Turn left and pick up the walk again, shortly after the 3h15min-point.

2   **Countryside and Fort St Philip** (12.3km/7.6mi; 3h; grade, equipment as main walk; access: 🚌 to Mahón, then 🚌 to Es Castell, or 🚐 to Es Castell). Pick up the main walk at the 2h55min-point (the military museum in the Plaça de S'Esplanada). Shortly after the 3h15min-point, at Cala Figuera, go up steps by the petrol depot and turn left to climb to the top of the hill. Cross the road, then follow the walk from the 28min-point back to the 2h55min-point. Return by 🚌 from Es Castell to Mahón, then 🚌 from Mahón, or 🚐 from Es Castell.

3   **Harbour** (4.5km/2.8mi; 1h05min; grade, equipment as main walk; access: 🚌 or 🚐 to Mahón, then 🚌 to Es Castell). Begin the walk at the 2h55min-point in the notes (the military museum in the Plaça de S'Esplanada) and follow it to the end.

4   **Mahón, countryside and Fort St Philip** (11.3km/7mi; 2h55min; grade, equipment as above; access: 🚌 or 🚐 to Mahón). Follow the main walk to the 2h55min-point. Turn left along Carrer Victori, and you will soon see the bus stop on your right. Return by 🚌 from Es Castell to Mahón, then 🚌 or 🚐 from Mahón.

This is perhaps the most interesting walk on the island. The outward part takes you through 18th-century Mahón, on through farming country, and then beside the coast, to bring you to the scant remains of what was once one of the Mediterranean's greatest fortresses: Fort St Philip. You return beside one of its longest and most beautiful harbours.

Start out in **Mahón** by standing with your back towards the **Monument to the Civil War Dead** in the **Plaça de S'Esplanada** (see town plan on pages 36-37). Leave the square by heading east along CARRER DE SES MORERES in the far right-hand corner. Turn right at the end along CARRER DE BASTIO, then walk down the hill of COSTA D'EN DEIA. Continue across the **Plaça Reial** into S'ARRAVALETA. Walk along the right-hand side of the **Plaça del Carmé** into the **Plaça del Príncep**. Take the right-hand road at the fork ahead, and make your way along the CAMI D'ES CASTELL. The *castell* was the great 16th-century fortress of

St Philip, which guarded the entrance to Mahón harbour. After passing the Andrea Doria flats at the end of the town, you will come to a large roundabout (**25min**). Keep straight ahead.

On your left is an arm of the harbour now known as **Cala Figuera** (**28min**). In former times the *cala* was called the 'English Creek', for a freshwater stream ran into the sea here, and ships of the Royal Navy would put in to take on water. Now it is petrol that is stored in the area. *(Shorter walk 1 leaves here.)* Almost opposite the *cala*, a road (the CAMI D'EN VERD) goes off to the right. *(Shorter walk 2 joins here.)* Follow this road for 50m/yds, looking for a narrow walled-in footpath on the left. Go along the footpath, then up steps to join the CAMI DE BINIATAP. Turn left. After a few metres/yards, ignore a track on the left, and follow your road round to the right. In four minutes ignore a tarmac road on the left leading to the houses of **Son Vilar**. As you walk along the Camí de Biniatap look out on your left for a large defensive tower adjacent to an old farmhouse (see panel on page 129). Ignore another road on the left, and two minutes later cross straight over the road which runs from Trepucó to Es Castell. Continue along a tarmac road past the Es Castell industrial estate *(Polígono industrial)*.

Some 10m/yds after passing Carrer d'es Fusters on the left the road forks (**50min**). Ignore the road on the left signposted to Punt Verd and follow a wide metalled road to the right. After 50m/yds turn left along a narrow walled-in track. After six minutes ignore a track on the left; seven minutes after that turn right at the next junction, ignoring firstly the Camí de Rafal on the left and in 10m/yds a narrow track on your right. You will see ahead of you a circle of RADIO MASTS. In five minutes pass a drive on the right, and soon you will come to the SANT LLUIS/ES CASTELL ROAD (Me-6). Cross over towards the white farmhouse shown on page 51 and follow the track to the left of it. In three minutes bear right when you reach a tarmac road. As you walk along this road you have a fine view of the military base of Sa Mola to your left. In six minutes ignore a lane on your left, and shortly pass the farm of SES AUBERTONAS. Next door is the military establishment with the aerial masts seen earlier. After you have passed the entrance to the base and the farm of Sant

Joan de Binissaida, turn left on to a wide dirt road (the CAMI DE SA TORRA) signposted 'HORTS DE BINISSAIDA'. Here look to your right, where between the trees you will see the sturdy tower of the old FORTIFIED FARMHOUSE shown on page 23 (**1h26min**). Follow this road for 600m/0.35mi, ignoring all side tracks, until you arrive in front of the large wooden gates of the Villa Eugenia. Turn left into a narrow walled-in track called CAMI DE SA CALA (actually part of the CAMI DE CAVALLS, mentioned on page 100). Where the grounds of the villa finish, turn right and leave the track by climbing through a gap in the wall. Follow a well-walked path across fields and through more gaps in walls towards the sea, arriving just to the left of a defensive tower built during the Napoleonic War, the **Torre d'en Penjat**.

Turn left and walk beside the sea (Picnic 2) for 10 minutes, until you reach another, older tower. To the right you can see where stone has been quarried to build these fortifications. Since everything on the island has been built of stone from time immemorial, you will frequently come across old quarries when walking and, near Ciutadella, some that have been developed as a tourist attraction (see Walk 22).

Make your way round or over the tower, and join a tarmac road which turns left to follow the edge of the beautiful **Cala de Sant Esteve**, known for a hundred years to British servicemen as St Stephen's Creek. Over the creek you can see all that remains of Fort St Philip. After Barbarossa had destroyed Mahón in 1535, the Emperor Charles V gave orders that a fort should be built on the south side of the harbour mouth. The work, entrusted to an Italian engineer named Juan Bautista Calvi, began in 1554. During the 18th century the British spent £1.5 million on strengthening its defences. However, during the Spanish occupation of the island from 1781-98, King Carlos III gave orders for its demolition; a curious act of unilateral disarmament which enabled General Sir Charles Stuart to retake the island without the loss of a single British life when the outbreak of the Napoleonic Wars made a Mediterranean base for the Royal Navy once again imperative.

On your left you will see the entrance to a small fort built to provide crossfire with Fort St Philip. Named after a great British general, it was known as the **Marlborough Redoubt**. In the final assault in 1781, a captain and 50 men withstood a French force of 700 men. It is said to be connected to Fort St Philip by a subterranean passage beneath the *cala*. The redoubt may be visited for a small fee. It is usually closed during the early afternoon. When you have explored the redoubt, continue round the *cala* as it bends to the right. When you have finally walked round the end of it, look carefully for a narrow footpath on your left by a clump of bamboo and climb it. This path (part of the Camí de Cavalls) is in fact one of the oldest roads on the island, built by the Romans; originally it continued to Mahón.

At the top of the path, stop and turn round before continuing your walk. From here you have a splendid view of the redoubt. Now bear left, ignore a track on your left, and walk to the junction with the Cf-2. Turn left again, and in four minutes you will come to a crossroads beside a CEMETERY (**2h17min**). Turn right now along the AVINGUDA DEL PORT into **Sol del Este**. Ignoring three roads on the left, follow the PASSEIG MARITIM round to the left until you come to the CAFETERIA SOL DEL ESTE. Turn right and walk towards the sea. The walk continues to the left now, but for Picnic 17 and an interesting detour, turn right until you come to a wall with stile which will give you access to the site of **Fort St Philip**. (You may explore as far as the barbed wire fence, but beyond, as you will see, the *zona militar* is still occupied by the Spanish Regiment of Artillery.) This is the setting for Picnic 17, a superb spot where you can watch the cruise liners entering and leaving the harbour.

Across the water can be seen the fortifications built on Sa Mola in the 1840s to replace Fort St Philip in giving protection to the harbour mouth. They were never finished. The large island in front of it is known as Illa del Llatzeret (Lazareto) and was used to house victims of the plague. The high walls, it was hoped, would prevent infection being blown into Mahón.

Retrace your steps to the end of the passage beside the Cafetería Sol del Este and carry on along the Passeig Maritim, rounding the headland and turning into **Cala Padera**. When you reach the restaurant SOL NACIENTE, go down steps, cross the tiny beach and walk up steps. On joining a tarmac road (CARRER XALOC), turn right. This takes you into CARRER GREGAL.

At the end of Carrer Gregal, at a wide asphalted area, turn right to some wooden steps. Go down these to the edge of the water and

Farm near the Sant Lluís/ Es Castell road

turn left. Walk along the wooden mooring platform for a few metres/yards, into **Cala Fonts**, the harbour of **Es Castell**. The name of the town has changed over the centuries. Having grown up as a settlement nestling in the shadow of Fort St Philip, it was first known as Philipstown. When the French attacked the fort in 1756, its houses gave them excellent cover. After the island was returned to Britain, orders were given for Philipstown to be demolished and a new town built further away. It was named Georgetown, in honour of King George III. Like Mahón, its architecture is similar to 18th-century English buildings. When Menorca reverted to Spain, the town was renamed Villa Real de San Carlos, in honour of one of the most enlightened monarchs of the century, Carlos III. Its name was shortened to Villa-Carlos, but is always referred to locally as Es Castell, from its proximity to Es Castell de Sant Felip — Fort St Philip.

Walk up the hill on the left of the harbour and keep straight ahead on the main street, CARRER STUART (named after General Stuart). Walk across the **Plaça de S'Esplanada** — once the parade ground of the British soldiery whose old barracks surround the square. Now one has been turned into housing, while the **Cuartel de Cala Corp** (**2h55min**) is the military museum. *(Shorter walks 2 and 3 begin here; Shorter walk 4 ends here.)* Continuing along Carrer Stuart, you pass the street leading to the smaller harbour, Cala Corb. Carrer Stuart ends at the junction with Carrer Fontanilles. Cross over and bear diagonally right into CARRER AGAMENON. Follow Carrer Agamenón past the hotel as far as a turning circle beside a yellow house. Turn left along an unmade road and 10m/yds further on bear right on a narrow path. Where the path divides twice, choose the right hand fork each time, so that you head for the cliff edge and follow the path across a field, beside the harbour. Ahead, the lovely red building is the Hotel del Almirante, named after the admiral Lord Collingwood, commander-in-chief of the Mediterranean fleet, who lived here during the Napoleonic Wars. In seven minutes, when the path divides, keep right, descending to pass in front of some white houses; then take steps down to the HARBOUR ROAD (**3h15min**).

Turn left and follow this road round **Cala Figuera**. *(Shorter walk 1 rejoins here; Shorter walk 2 climbs up past the petrol depot.)* Continuing beside **Mahón harbour**, after half an hour you will be at the COMMERCIAL DOCK. Again referring to the town plan, climb steps on the left up through **Parc Rochina**. Turn right at the top, up CARRER SANT CRIST, then go left into CARRER NOU. At the end you return to the **Plaça Reial**. Turn right and climb back up COSTA D'EN DEIA, turning left at the crossroads to follow SES MORERES back to the **Plaça de S'Esplanada** (**4h**).

Walk 5: TREPUCO

See map on reverse of touring map; see also photograph on page 39 and drawings on pages 12 and 13

Distance: 5.3km/3.3mi; 1h15min

Grade: easy

Equipment: comfortable shoes of any sort, sunhat, raingear, suncream

How to get there and return: as Walk 1, page 32 (park in the Plaça de S'Esplanada)

The prehistoric settlement at Trepucó has a double advantage: it's near to Mahón and has the largest monuments on Menorca. The original excavation of the site was undertaken in 1931 by Dr Margaret Murray and a team from Cambridge University.

Golden Farm, seen from the distance on Walks 4, 5 and 6: it is thought that Admiral Lord Nelson stayed here for five days in 1799, and popular legend has it that Lady Hamilton accompanied him.

TREPUCO

The monuments of Trepucó were built during the second millennium BC, at about the time Moses was leading the children of Israel out of Egypt. The first people to see them in modern times believed that only giants could have lifted the huge stones and attributed them to Homer's Cyclops, hence the term 'cyclopean' which is sometimes used as an alternative to 'megalithic' (Greek for 'big stones') to describe this kind of architecture.

In this photograph, the *taula* (the largest on Menorca) rises in front of the massive *talayot*.

In the adjacent field to the west, part of the village has been excavated (see illustration on page 13), revealing amongst much else a 'hypostyle chamber', with typical pillar and one roofing slab still in place.

Start out in **Mahón** by standing with your back towards the **Monument to the Civil War Dead** in the **Plaça de S'Esplanada** (see town plan on pages 36-37). Leave the square by heading east along CARRER DE SES MORERES in the right-hand corner. Then take the first turning on the right, ES COS DE GRACIA. In 300m/yds you cross Carrer Santiago Ramon i Cajal and, after another 200m/yds, pass two more roads on your left. Now referring to the back of the touring map, bear slightly right, to the roundabout. Cross over the busy dual carriageway and keep straight ahead on a country lane (Me-4) signposted 'RESIDENCIA DE TREPUCO', soon passing the CEMETERY on the left. Ignore Camí d'en Barrotes on the right, a road on the left, and in a while Camí de Binitalfa straight ahead. Follow your road round to the left, and soon you will arrive at more crossroads. Turn right to the site of **Trepucó** (**27min**).

Twice during the 18th century Britain briefly lost control of Menorca to the French — in 1756 (to the Duc de Richelieu) and in 1782 (to the Duc de Crillon, at the head of a joint French and Spanish army). While he was besieging Fort St Philip, the Duc de Crillon mounted his artillery on the *talayot* of Trepucó and built the thick defensive wall which still surrounds the site, using stones from nearby *talayots*. Yet it is the gigantic *taula* which has pride of place here. The stone circle surrounding it led the first English historian of Menorca, John Armstrong, to conclude (erroneously) that it was the work of Druids. It is the largest on the island. You can find out more about these monuments on pages 12-13.

When you leave the site, turn left and, on reaching the crossroads, take the road opposite (signposted 'CAMI D'EN VERD') and bear right. This pleasant country lane is some 1.3km/0.8mi long and will bring you to the Mahón/Es Castell road at Cala Figuera. En route, in about ten minutes, you will be able to look along the road and across the harbour directly at a lovely red house proudly standing on top of the far cliff. It is Golden Farm, linked in legend with Admiral Lord Nelson.

Just before the end of the Camí d'en Verd you pass a CAVE on your right (**45min**). The lane passes next through what was once a QUARRY and brings you to the MAHON/ES CASTELL ROAD. You now have a choice of ways. Either follow the directions below, which take you through the town, or, if you prefer to walk beside the harbour, turn to Walk 4 and follow it from shortly after the 3h15min-point to its end (page 52).

Turn left at the T-junction (**50min**) and go up the hill to Mahón. Keep straight ahead at the ROUNDABOUT, between a petrol station and the Andrea Doria flats. Continue along CAMI D'ES CASTELL for 200m/yds, and turn left on CARRER DE SANT MANUEL at the crossroads. Then take the third turning on the right, CARRER DE LA INFANTA. Follow it past three streets on the left. You come to CARRER DE GRACIA (see town plan). Turn left along it, but in a few metres/yards keep right along CARRER SANTIAGO RAMON I CAJAL, passing the **Parc d'Es Freginal** on the right. At the next junction (**1h10min**) turn right and follow ES COS DE GRACIA back to its junction with CARRER DE SES MORERES. Turn left to the **Plaça de S'Esplanada** (**1h15min**).

WALK 6: ST STEPHEN'S CREEK AND THE BINISSAIDA COAST

See map on reverse of the touring map; see also photographs pages 23, 49, 53 and 100 (right)

Distance: 11km/7mi; 3h 05min

Grade: easy

Equipment: comfortable footwear, sunhat, suncream, long trousers, long sleeves, rainwear, picnic (or have lunch in one of the restaurants in Sol del Este or Es Castell), plenty of water

How to get there and return: 🚌 to/from Es Castell (you will probably have to get a bus to Mahón first) or 🚗 to Es Castell. There is a large car park beside the Me-2 close to the bus stop and football ground.

Shorter walk: St Stephen's Creek (7km/4.4mi; 1h45min; grade, equipment, access as main walk). Follow the main walk to the 45min- point, but instead of going through the gap, turn right and walk past the tower and across the fields for 200m/yds, to a gap in a broken wall. This gives on to a walled-in track, the Camí de Sa Cala. Turn right, following the main walk from the 2h05min-point.

Here is a most enjoyable walk along the beautiful coast which runs south from the entrance to Mahón harbour, in a region filled with historical associations. Since it partly overlaps with Walk 4, additional information can be found on pages 48-52.

Begin the walk at the BUS STOP in **Es Castell** near the parish church on the main MAHON/ES CASTELL Road (Me-2) and turn left in the direction of Sant Lluís. Pass the fine CHURCH on the left and a splendid red house on the right before coming to a crossroads. Keep straight ahead here and pass a CEMETERY on the left (**12min**).

If after very heavy rain the depression in the road is flooded, you will be grateful for the raised causeway at the side, as doubt-less the Redcoats would have been on their way to Fort St Philip which lay at the end of this road, where the *zona militar* is now. Turn right at the junction and in six minutes, at the top of a hill, ignore a track to the right and look ahead. Furthest away, on top of the cliff, is the Torre d'en Penjat, a watchtower built during the Napoleonic War, and before it and to its left is the Marl-borough Redoubt, built to provide crossfire with Fort St Philip. Some 60m/yds further on, fork right down a path beneath power lines. Lower down, notice its extraordinarily fine cobbled surface, which in all likelihood was laid as long ago as the time of the Roman occupation of Menorca (see panel page 65). At the bottom, turn right and walk round **Cala de Sant Esteve**, pass-ing the entrance to the **Marlborough Redoubt** (**26min**).

At the end of the creek follow the road uphill to where, at the end of a small parking area, a path to the left goes through bushes, to steps which take you to the top of a little tower. But *take care,* because there is a large hole where once the roof was. Keep climbing and follow a narrow path in the direction of the **Torre d'en Penjat**. As you do so, notice on your left how the cliff has been quarried away to provide stone to build the fort. At the end of a solid wall going down from the Torre d'en Penjat to the water's edge, go through a GAP (**45min**) and down steps. *(But for the Shorter walk, turn right here.)* On your right you will see the VILLA EUGENIA. Turn to page 79 to read of the unfortunate experience of Admiral Byng in these waters. For the next 37 minutes you are going to walk between the sea on your left and a wall on your right (unless the owners of Villa Eugenia have blocked off the coastal path now that there is an alternative route inland, in which case you will have to follow the Camí de Sa Cala/Camí de Cavalls to Binissaida; see violet lines on the map).

Three minutes beyond the gap you will come to a place where, for a few minutes, the path squeezes between bushes and the wall. Beyond the last of the bushes are some old buildings, and above you on the right a second villa. After another ten minutes you reach a tiny creek, **Es Caló d'es Vi Blanc**. A *botador* (stile) in the facing right hand corner provides safe way over the wall. Then the path bears slightly left, climbs a little hill, goes through a gap in a wall four minutes later and then bears right. Continue as before, with the sea to your left and the wall to your right, ignoring any gaps in the wall leading into fields.

Twelve minutes later you will come to the end of a headland, where the resort of S'Algar is facing you across the water. Here you pass the quaint building shown below, 'NUMBER 68' (**1h22min**). Judging by the slipway, it began life as a boathouse, although then it must have had a wider entrance. Here you turn right and leave the coast. The path goes through a gateway in a wall and into a small field full of bushes. It twists to the right, passes in front of a dere-  lict troglodytic dwelling and carries on for a while beside a wall (heading back the way you came), before swinging left and zigzagging upwards between bushes.

After five minutes, at the top of the cliff, go through a gateway and keep ahead at the side of a wall. In two minutes,

'Number 68', where the walk leaves the coast

ignore a gap in the wall on your left with a red-arrowed path going through it. Keep straight ahead in the same direction you have been going, still at the right of the wall. At the end of this field go through quite a wide gap in a wall and into another field. Cross this and go on into a third field, where the gateway has a red dot on a stone on the left. Now the path changes direction: it heads off diagonally right across this field. Along this section you will see red dots on stones from time to time. Leave this field in the far right-hand corner by taking the gate on the right (red arrow pointing back the way you have come). Again cross the next field diagonally, as the path zigzags between bushes (more red dots). Once through the gap in the far right-hand corner of this field, the path again changes direction and meanders over towards the farmhouse ahead. Go through a gap in the wall, which may or not be closed with an improvised barrier, into a track and turn left, away from the house (**Binissaida; 1h42min**).

Beyond another gateway, ignore the Camí de Cavalls on the left* and follow a tarred road on the right. In 50m/yds, at a T-junction, turn left towards another fine farmhouse. Notice to the left of it that it has its own CHAPEL, even equipped with a bell. Next you will pass on your right the fine FORTIFIED FARMHOUSE shown on page 23 (see also panel page 129). Five minutes beyond this farmhouse, turn right into Horts de Binissaida along CAMÍ DE SA TORRA. In another five minutes, ignore a road to the right and keep ahead on the wider one, to arrive in a further five minutes before the gates of the house seen earlier, VILLA EUGENIA. Turn left along a track called CAMÍ DE SA CALA, which is part of the CAMÍ DE CAVALLS (see panel on page 100). In four minutes you reach the end of the Villa Eugenia property, by a gap where the wall has been broken down (**2h05min**). *(The Shorter walk rejoins here.)*

Continue to follow the Camí de Sa Cala down to the end of **Cala de Sant Esteve** (St Stephen's Creek; photograph page 100) and join the tarmac road. Turn left and cross the end of the *cala*, but leave the road when you come to a clump of bamboo and go up the little Roman path. At the top bear left and turn left at the T-junction. Soon you will be back beside the CEMETERY (**2h36min**), where motorists will find their cars.

Pick up the notes for Walk 4 on page 51 now, and follow it from the 2h17min-point to the 2h55min-point —the **Plaça de S'Esplanada**, the square in the centre of **Es Castell**. Walk ahead until you come to CARRER VICTORI. Turn left, pass the church, and the bus stop is to your right (**3h05min**).

---

*This makes a pleasant link with Walk 12; in 10 minutes it would bring you to the 1h08min-point in that walk.

Walk 7: TORELLO AND TALATI DE DALT

See map on reverse of touring map; see also photographs on pages 1, 12, 13, 39

Distance: about 13km/8mi; 3h35min

Grade: moderate

Equipment: comfortable footwear, sunhat, raingear, suncream, picnic, plenty of water

How to get there and return: 🚌 or 🚗 to Mahón; as Walk 1, page 32 (park in the Esplanade Square)

Shorter walk: Torelló (about 10.5km/6.5mi; 2h55min; grade, equipment, access as main walk). Follow the main walk to the 1h36min-point, then turn right and pick up the notes at the 2h15min-point to end the walk, *omitting Talatí de Dalt*.

In 1956, 'Torelló' first appeared on the archaeological map of Menorca, when a very large and magnificent mosaic pavement featuring flowers, birds and animals was discovered. It has since been identified as the floor of an early Christian church. Talatí de Dalt, too, is famed among enthusiasts of Menorcan archaeology as one of the most beautiful of talayotic village sites. This walk also visits two other interesting *talayots*, and so is an excellent way for the visitor to see some of Menorca's prehistoric legacy.

Start out by facing the **Monument to the Civil War Dead** in the **Plaça de S'Esplanada** (see town plan on pages 36-37). Leave the square by the street in the far right-hand corner, CARRER VASSALLO (it is the airport road). Pass the barracks built in the 18th century to house British soldiers and keep ahead at a large roundabout. After passing a sports stadium, you will see ahead a dual carriageway and roundabout. Just before this, turn left along a narrow lane and in 30m/yds turn right and go up steps on to the BRIDGE OVER THE DUAL CARRIAGEWAY. Where the bridge divides, turn left. At the bottom of the bridge, turn round and walk back to the roundabout. Follow the dual carriageway to the right towards Sant Lluís for 100m/yds, then turn right again in the direction of Llucmaçanes and rejoin the little lane. You now follow this lane (CAMI DE BAIX) for just over 1km/ 0.75mi. Ignore the turning to the right by No 27.

After an S-bend round a DAIRY FARM, you come to a straight stretch of road. Looking right you may see the fine farmhouse of Sa Cudia, almost hidden behind its imposing palm trees. In a few metres/yards you come to a narrow, walled-in crossing track (**28min**). Turn right and follow this track for another 1km/ 0.5mi. Fortunately the drystone walls are sufficiently low to afford a good view of the fields. In them you will see sheds built of loose stones — the way the people of Menorca have been building for three thousand years (see panel on page 123).

At the end of the track (**43min**) you come to a junction with a metalled road. Turn right. In 350m/yds you meet the MAIN

ROAD from Mahón to the airport at Sant Climent. Cross this road and carry on towards the industrial estate (*Polígono industrial*). Walk along the edge of the estate for 200m/yds. Just before the road bends right, turn left down a narrow lane, the CAMI VELL DE SANT CLIMENT. Fork left when you are in sight of the farmhouse shown on page 62, **Curnia Vey**, and pass the splendid *talayot* of **Curnia** on your left. This is the first megalithic building visitors see on leaving the airport.

After exploring the *talayot,* carry on past a QUARRY and scrapyard, and soon you come to a junction with the road joining the Mahón to Ciutadella highway to the airport (Me-14; **1h**). Cross straight over, heading diagonally left. Soon you will enjoy a fine view across fields to the *talayot* at Torelló. Beyond a handful of houses the road is unsurfaced, then metalled again beyond a farm, When you join a road beside the AIRPORT LANDING LIGHTS, turn right for 20m/yds, then left on a lane signed to the 'EL SERENO' restaurant. Ignore a lane on the left in 250m/yds and, in a further 200m/yds, you will arrive at the towering *talayot* of **Torelló** (**1h 17min**), unusual in that it possesses an entrance. Continue along the lane. To your left is the omnipresent Monte Toro. In six minutes turn right along a short track towards a large shed-like structure, signposted 'Basílica des Fornàs de Torelló'. It covers the mosaic floor of a church built during the Roman empire. The flowers and animals are African (what a wonderful lion), suggesting that the Menorcan church at this time maintained close links with the church in North Africa, where the great St Augustine was bishop of Hippo.

Return to the lane, turn right and

TALATI DE DALT
Talatí de Dalt has all the usual features of these prehistoric Menorcan villages — caves, hypostyle chambers, *talayot,* and *taula.* And all this in an idyllic setting (Picnic 5). In the absence of metals and large trees, the lives of the ancient villagers were dominated by stones. Looking about you, it is apparent how all their building was done with them, but so also was their hunting and fighting (see opposite).

PREHISTORIC WEAPONRY

The weapon of the Balearic islanders of pre-history was the sling shot. So skilled were they, that they were in great demand as mercenaries for several centuries. When the Carthaginian general Mago sailed into Mahón harbour in 206 BC, thereby bequeathing it his name, it was to impress 2000 Menorcan slingers into his army. (It is possible that the very name 'Balearic' comes from the Greek word 'ballein' which means 'to sling'.) Each soldier carried three slings of different sizes, to be used according to the distance, like golf clubs. The stones they used generally weighed about 500g (about a pound), and it was claimed that

Photographs: taula *enclosure and* talayot *at the site of Talatí de Dalt (top); the* taula *and nearby standing stones (above)*

they were accurate up to 600 paces. Boys were trained from early childhood. Their mothers would place the children's meals up in a tree, and the youngsters had to knock them down with a sling shot. Or go hungry. Their skeletal remains show remarkable development of the shoulder-blade and upper humerus, the

latter also being bowed. Having served with the Carthaginian armies, Menorcan slingers later saw service with the Roman legions. Julius Caesar refers to the part they played in his defeat of the Gauls at Alesia in 52 BC.

continue in your original direction, soon passing another old quarry on the right and the El Sereno restaurant on your left (open only after 8pm). In 0.5km/0.3mi, at a T-junction (**1h36min**), turn left along a track. Ignore turnings to the right (after 250m/yds and 200m/yds further on), and follow the track for 0.7km/0.4mi to a T-junction with a metalled road. Shortly before the T-junction there is a short section where the track still retains its original Roman paving (see panel page 65). Turn left, and very soon you will see a sign, 'Taula de Talatí'. **Talatí de Dalt** (**1h55min**) is the site of the prehistoric village shown on pages 1 and 12-13. An entrance fee is payable, but it is well worth it (see www.menorcaweb.net/talati). What a marvellous place it is for a picnic (Picnic 5), with ample shade and enough room to get out of the way of other sightseers.

When you leave the talayotic settlement (**2h**), turn right, and after a few metres/yards turn right again, to retrace your steps to the T-junction at the 1h36min-point (**2h15min**). *Now you have a choice.* You can return to town by following Walk 8 from the 2h47min-point (page 64), but this means going back over much of your outward route. I think it's preferable to join Walk 3 (even if you've done it already). Turn *left* at this junction, following signs for Mahón and Ciutadella. Pass under the Me-14 connecting the Me-1 with the airport and, in 150m/yds, keep left at the fork. Meeting the Me-1, either take the track directly opposite or the one 180m/yds to the right. Both descend to a T-junction by a MEADOW (**2h35min**), where you join Walk 3. Turning right, use the notes from the 1h25min-point on page 46 to walk back to the **Plaça de S'Esplanada** (**3h35min**).

Curnia Vey farmhouse: not only is the track to it metalled, but the farm now stands isolated just south of the perimeter of Mahón's enlarged industrial estate.

Walk 8: AN ARCHAEOLOGICAL RAMBLE

See map on reverse of touring map; see also photographs on pages 1, 12-13, 39, 60-61 and opposite

Distance: 13km/8mi; 3h20min

Grade: easy

Equipment: comfortable footwear, sunhat, raingear, suncream, picnic, plenty of water

How to get there: 🚌 to Alaior or Cala'n Porter, then 🚕 taxi to Torralba d'en Salort. You may wish to leave your car at the end of the walk; if so, park beneath the Esplanade Square, then go on by bus as above.

To return: 🚌 or 🚕 from Mahón

Since this walk takes in two major prehistoric settlements, two additional important *talayots*, two *navetas*, the mosaic floor of a Roman church, and follows what was the main road across the island until Sir Richard Kane built his new highway early in the 18th century, it is clearly a 'must' for the amateur historian and archaeology buff.

Start out at the prehistoric settlement of **Torralba d'en Salort**, inhabited for two millennia from 1800 BC. Hoskin and Waldron suggest that the *taula* precinct is the most beautiful prehistoric monument in the Balearics, and date it from 890 BC. At the foot of the *taula* were found a small stone altar and a bronze bull. Nearby is the **Pou de Na Patarra**, a huge well dating from 800 BC, with nine flights of steps leading down, and a handrail hewn out of the rock. At the time of writing it was closed to the public and not signposted, but do look to see if it has re-opened.

Some 20m/yds beyond the site car park, turn left on a track by the side of Torralba d'en Salort farm. This track, the CAMÍ D'ALCAIDUS, was once the main road across Menorca; it's continuation, via Alaior, is now a busy road. Proceed through gorgeous farming country for 2km/1.3mi, until you pass on your right the drive to SANTA ELISABET (**39min**), then SANT RAFAEL on your left. Ignore a track to the right here. In five minutes you come to a tarmac road and, when you do, look out for two picturesque old wells — one on your left with a wheel and buckets, and another on your right. Notice too the curious single standing stone inscribed '90 ANYS' (years). Follow the road round to the left. Where you pass beneath power lines there is a road on your right, but ignore that for the moment, because here you make a short detour to two *navetas*. Turn left and walk 50m/yds to the main road. Cross with care and walk along the road opposite. The well-signposted *navetas* of **Rafal Rubí** (**56min**) were built in the talayotic period as burial chambers.

When you leave the *navetas,* walk back along the lane to the main road and cross over. This time take the road on the left when you reach the junction, going under power lines. Keep

WELLS

On Menorca it sometimes it seems that no matter where you look, you see a well (*pou* in Menorcan).

Perhaps that is an exaggeration, but they are very plentiful and you will see many, beside paths and in fields.

The simple stone structures surrounding them, sometimes adding drinking troughs, are often curiously attractive and the wells add much interest to the scenery.

Photograph: well near the farm of Sant Rafael

going along this road for 1.5km/1mi, until you reach the hamlet of Algendar de Sa Costa, and turn left at the crossroads. In 20 minutes you will come to a sign reading 'TAULA DE TALATI' and another prehistoric village, **Talatí de Dalt** (**1h43min**; Picnic 5). Walk 7 will tell you more about the inhabitants of these townships.

Continue along the road in the same direction for 100 metres/yards, then turn right along a track, the CAMI VELL D'ALAIOR ('Old Alaior Road'). A little way along this track you come upon a section of very fine paving — a clue to the Roman origins of this road. Of course, linking as it does so many Bronze Age towns, the way itself predates by far the Roman era. Five minutes along the track, look on your right for a narrow path which leads to some CAVES. Some 200m/yds further on you are directly beneath the airport flight path.

About now ignore a path to the left and, in 200m/yds, turn right at a T-junction signposted to a restaurant, 'EL SERENO', along a metalled lane, the CAMI DE TORELLO (**2h03min**). You pass this restaurant after 10 minutes (it is only open after 8pm). Soon afterwards, beyond an old QUARRY, turn left along a short track bearing the sign '**Basílica des Fornàs de Torelló**'. This brings you to a Roman mosaic pavement, believed to be the floor of a Christian church. (See notes on page 60.)

Return to the lane and carry on in the same direction for six minutes, when you will reach the *talayot* of **Torelló** (also called 'Torellonet Vell'; **2h22min**). It is unusual in that it has an entrance leading to a chamber on top. In 200m/yds ignore a lane on the right (the Camí de Mussulá), and in three more minutes emerge on a road beside the AIRPORT LANDING LIGHTS. Turn right, but after 20m/yds turn left on a lane; it is metalled at first, but after a farm reverts to an older and simpler state for a short time. After 10 minutes cross a main road and go along a facing lane (CAMI VELL DE SANT CLIMENT), pass a scrapyard and old quarry, and ignore a turning on the right.

Now you will see the fine **Curnia** *talayot* on your right (**2h43min**). Keep ahead past some large CAVES. As you approach a T-junction, you have the view of Curnia Vey farmhouse shown on page 62. Turn right at the junction. Follow the lane to the right and join a road. Turn right. On your left is Mahón's large industrial estate (*Polígono industrial*).

Walk towards the main road, but turn left just short of it, and follow the quieter road (CARRER DE ARTRUTX) beside the estate into Mahón. At the end of the industrial estate, cross the DUAL CARRIAGEWAY (**3h11min**) and keep ahead. Beyond a sports ground, you will come to a ROUNDABOUT. Keep straight ahead (although you will probably have to make a short detour to cross the road) and follow CARRER VASSALLO straight to the **Plaça de S'Esplanada** in **Mahón** (**3h 20min**).

ROMAN ROADS

Wheeled vehicles need smooth, flat surfaces if they are to work efficiently. An uneven surface not only gives an uncomfortable ride, but every bump acts as a brake on the vehicle's progress. The Romans managed to obtain remarkably smooth surfaces by taking meticulous care over the shaping and laying of the cobbles with which their roads were surfaced.

The 140 km of roads they built on Menorca were no exception. Today most of the old Roman roads are buried beneath later resurfacing. But not quite everywhere, and a few stretches of Roman paving still lie on the surface, and you will walk over several of them as you follow the routes in this book. The best and longest stretch is to be found on Picnic 8, part of the path leading up to the ruins of the summer palace of the Moorish king of Menorca at the time of the Reconquest. Formerly there had been a Roman fortress here. Other lengths of Roman paving will be encountered on Walks 3, 4, 6, 7 and 8.

Photograph: Roman road at Santa Agueda (Picnic 8)

Walk 9: THREE WALKS NEAR THE VALLEY OF EGYPT

Walk a: Sant Llorenç to Binimatzoc (7km/4.5mi; 1h40min; easy)
Walk b: Sant Llorenç to Ejipte (2.8km/1.7mi; 50min; easy)
Walk c: Sant Llorenç and Puig Menor (6km/3.7mi; 1h35min; moderate)
Equipment: comfortable footwear, sunhat, suncream, raingear, picnic, plenty of water

Access/return: drive along the Camí d'en Kane until you are nearly level with Alaior. You will come to a crossroads where one turning is to Alaior and the other is signposted to Camí de Binixems. Follow the latter road for about 3 kilometres (2 miles), when you will come to a junction with the Camí d'en Rossi on the left. Either park here or continue along the Camí de Binixems for another 500m/yds until you are nearly at the church of Sant Llorenç and you will see a small clearing on your right. Park here or by the church (but avoid on Sundays).

Walking in inland Menorca often presents problems of access, as explained in the article about 'gates' on page 42. Walk 9b is a good example, but before you give up and turn back, *do* look to see if there is a stile not too far distant from the blocked gate.

Start Walk a at the little church of **Sant Llorenç** by walking to the junction with the Camí d'en Rossi and turning along this road. Follow it until you arrive at a Y-junction (**15min**), where you turn right. The tarmac ends (**23min**) and you go through a gate, keeping left at a fork in 50m/yds. In three minutes go through another gate. The track loops round the bottom of the hill below the ESTANCIA DE SANT PERE for ten minutes, before you go through a gateway (**36min**). Three minutes later fork left to avoid BINIMATZOC farmhouse, and in four minutes go through a gate. The track now runs through trees. At the next fork go right, ignoring a gateway on the left. Soon you will have a good view over the last field before the Me-7 road, and unless you are going to pick up transport there, little is to be gained by walking further (**50min**).

Retrace your steps now. Ignore the gateway on the right, walk through woodland for a couple of minutes, then go through a gate and, four minutes after that, turn right at the T-junction where the track on the left goes to Binimatzoc farm. In three minutes go through another gate (**59min**). On top of a hill on your left you can see the farm of SANT PERE, and your track will loop round the bottom of the hill. After ten minutes, when you are about three-quarters of the way round the loop, you go through yet another gate. In three minutes bear right, ignoring the track on the left which goes to the farm (**1h13min**). A minute later you pass through the final gate and the track becomes a metalled lane. In eight minutes keep straight ahead at a junction, ignoring a road to the right, on what is now a wider road. You pass the entrance to ESTANCIA DE SANTA MARGALIDA in another

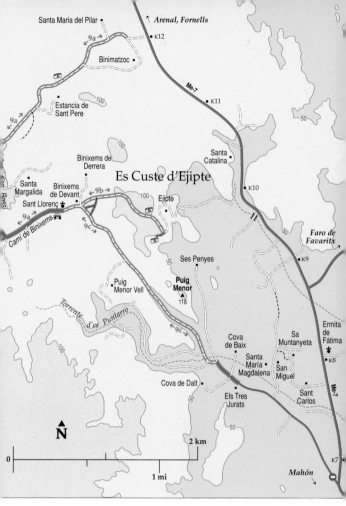

seven minutes (**1h29min**) and after a similar interval you will come to the junction with Camí de Binixems. Turn left for 500m/yds to arrive at **Sant Llorenç** (**1h40min**).

Start Walk b by making your way to the little church (*ermita*) of **Sant Llorenç** and continue along the lane for five minutes, until you come to a crossroads beside the farm of BINIXEMS DE DEVANT. Your ongoing route is straight ahead, following a track through a gate and across a field. This gate is is usually locked, so look for a stile in the wall anywhere from 20m to 100m/yds downhill (it keeps moving!). Once over the stile, walk up the right-hand side of the field and join a path. Follow it across the next field. At the top it will bend left and go downhill. Cross a field at the bottom, to join your ongoing track and turn right. *Mark this junction carefully;* you will need it on your return.)

After about 15min you will come to another locked gate.

Climb over the wall to the right of it (or look for another stile). As you go forward now, you will see the **Ejipte** farmhouse on your left and, just before the track bends sharply left to begin to descend, the valley of **Ses Penyes**. The hill of Puig Menor stands out on the right. Do not follow the track downhill, but continue to walk round to the right, for the view over the GORGE (**25min**).

Turn round now and retrace your steps. After 15 minutes you should see on the other side of a little field the path that will take you up and round to the right and bring you back to the stile in the wall. Once back on the lane, turn right to return to **Sant Llorenç** (**50min**).

Start Walk c at the church of **Sant Llorenç** and continue along the lane for five minutes, until you come to a crossroads beside the farm of BINIXEMS DE DEVANT. Turn right and follow

The Ejipte farmhouse in Es Custe d'Ejipte

the lane downhill. In ten minutes pass the entrance to PUIG MENOR VELL farm on your right.

At the bottom of the hill ignore a farm entrance on the right, and in 100m/yds turn left at a T-junction. Walk beside a stream for another 100m/yds, then turn right. No doubt you will see signs indicating that this area is private hunting ground (*caza*), and although a handful of cars may pass, they belong to the land-owners — the road running ahead to the Me-7, is usually closed to all other motorists. So you can enjoy the flora and birdsong of this gentle countryside in peace.

Pass between the farms of COVA DE DALT (Upper Cova) and COVA DE BAIX (Lower Cova) and lastly that of the three Councillors — ELS TRES JURATS. Can you see the rocks that gave the farm its name on your right in solemn contemplation (**45min**)?

The rest of the way from here to its junction with the Me-7 has little of interest, and unless you are intending to pick up transport there I recommend you turn round now and retrace your steps uphill back to **Sant Llorenç** (**1h35min**).

Right, from top to bottom, some Menorcan flora (see page 18): convolvulus, fig, olive, juniper and Pistacia lentiscus

Walk 10: MONTE TORO

Distance: 13.8km/8.6mi; 3h35min

Grade: strenuous, with an overall ascent of about 350m/1150ft

Equipment: comfortable footwear, sunhat, raingear, suncream, picnic, plenty of water

How to get there and return: 🚌 to Alaior or 🚍 to Es Mercadal (park in the town centre), then 🚌 to Alaior
To return: 🚌 or 🚍 from Es Mercadal

Shorter walk: Es Mercadal — Monte Toro — Es Mercadal (7km/4.3mi; 2h20min; equipment and grade as above (ascent of 300m/1000ft); access: 🚌 or 🚍 to Es Mercadal). From Es Mercadal walk back to the main Mahón/Ciutadella road (Me-1) and turn left towards Mahón. Once out of the town, turn left along the first road you come to: the Camí d'en Kane, or 'Kane's Road'. Follow it uphill for 1km/0.6mi (about 20 minutes), then join the main walk at the 1h53min-point.

Alternative endings. The road up Mount Toro is very busy nowadays. You may be deterred by the final steep climb or by the traffic on a comparatively narrow road. Here are three alternative ways to finish the walk.

1 **Avoiding the climb to the summit and the traffic.** At the 1h53min-point, do not turn right, but continue along the Camí d'en Kane as it descends to Es Mercadal. Turn right at the junction with the Me-1 and follow the ring road round Es Mercadal until you come to the end of the Mount Toro road. Pick up the walk from the 3h30min-point.

2 **Avoiding the climb to the summit.** At the 2h16min-point, turn left and descend to Es Mercadal, following the directions given after the 2h50min-point.

3 **Avoiding some of the traffic.** Follow the walk until shortly after the 2h50min-point but, when you come back to the entrance to the farm of Rafal d'es Frares (your outward route), turn left. Turn right down the track just beyond the farmhouse and, when you reach the junction with the Camí d'en Kane, turn right and use the notes for Alternative ending 1 above.

E very visitor will wish to get to the summit of Monte Toro, Menorca's loftiest hill (at 358m/1175ft, it just merits its name 'mountain'). The easiest way is to drive up. For the energetic, this walk provides an enjoyable alternative, combining an interesting country walk with an easier climb (at least to the 200m contour), than the road from Es Mercadal offers.

The town of Alaior is the third largest on Menorca. It was founded soon after the Reconquest in 1304 by King James II of Mallorca, on the site of the farmhouse of Ihalor. Some claim it to be the prettiest town on the island. The parish church of Santa Eulalia, fortified in 1558 after both Mahón and Ciutadella had been sacked by Turkish pirates, and the 17th-century Franciscan convent are of special interest. Alaior is best known for its ice cream, but shoes and cheese are made here too.

The BUS STOP in **Alaior** is in CARRER SANT JOAN BAPTISTA DE LA SALLE, in front of a park and playground. Facing the park, **begin the walk** by turning left, then turning right along the street running along the left-hand side of the park, CARRER MESTRE DURAN. The large building ahead dates from 1624. Originally a

The convent on Monte Toro, with its tower and chapel (above), statue of Christ (right) and the entrance (far right)

Franciscan convent, its pink church was dedicated to San Diego (St James). The local people refer to it as Sa Lluna, and it has now been converted to housing. Turn left in front of it along CARRER LES ESCOLES, then turn right and pass its entrance — turn in to look at the picturesque cloister.

Turn right and follow CARRER SANT DIEGO along its west wall, forking right at the end to go downhill. Turn left at the end, then fork right up CARRER COSTA D'ES POU. Bear right along CARRER DEL BISBE GONYALONS. At the top of the hill cross over CARRER D'ES PORRASSAR VELL and go straight ahead up CARRER DE SES NUVIES. At the top of the hill, Santa Eulalia's church is on your right. Turn right and walk in front of the church along CARRER DES RETXATS. Continue round until this joins CARRER DE SES GUIXES. Turn right, and in 50m/yds you are back at CARRER D'ES PORRASSAR VELL, by a palm tree. Turn left along the side of a tiny square, the **Plaça Espanya**, at the end of which you turn right into ES CAMI NOU. Pass a small garden with a playground and the CHURCH beside it (**16min**), and you have now crossed Alaior.

Turn left along a track at the back of the church. Ignore the first track to the left in 100m/yds, but in two minutes turn left along the second one, CAMI D'ES MIGJORN. In ten minutes go over a crossing track and pass the ESTANCIA D'EN AGUSTI. Seven minutes later again keep straight ahead, when an obviously more used track goes once more to the left. The track that you are on is the continuation of the one followed in Walk 8 — the main road linking the towns before Kane's road was built. After going under power lines you begin to walk through woodland. Ignore any tracks leading to farms or houses and, when you come out of the wood, go under power lines, cross over a stream and turn right at a T-junction (turning left would bring you to the main

Peu del Toro, a farmhouse passed on the descent from Monte Toro

road). At the time of writing there was a sign here, with the picture of a cow and the words 'Es Fasse' (**1h08min**).

Some 14 minutes after the T-junction you meet another junction, this time with a metalled road. This is the Camí d'en Kane, which from here to Es Mercadal follows the same line as the older road. Turn left and follow it for half an hour, passing three large farms: S'Astansia, Bini Llobet and S'Aranjassa. After the last of these the road goes downhill and bends to the left. Ignore a track to the right on the bend which leads to the farm of Sant Joan de la Creu, but within 50m/yds turn right through a gate (**1h53min**). *(The Shorter walk joins here.)* Climb a track past the drive to Son Carlos farm and in 12 minutes turn right towards the farm of Rafal d'es Frares. Go through a gate, and follow the track round to the left. At the end of the track, turn left at a T-junction along a tarmac drive, passing to the left of the farmhouse. Go through a gateway and walk up the side of a little valley, go over a cattle grid and join the road from Es Mercadal to Monte Toro (**2h16min**).

Turn right and in 200m/yds pass the KM2 marker. The road winds up the hillside. It is just about wide enough for you to keep out of the way of traffic, and occasionally you may be able to take a short-cut. It will take you about 45 minutes to climb to the summit of **Monte Toro** (**2h50min**). The 17th-century convent buildings house a cafeteria and toilets, as well as a gift shop. Outside, the statue of Christ gazes a little forlornly, I fancy, at the emblems of the more recent gods of the 21st century.

Your descent is very much quicker! Keep to the side of the road, facing the oncoming traffic, and you should be at the roundabout at the foot of the hill in 40 minutes (**3h30min**). Go straight over the roundabout and enter **Es Mercadal**. You will come to a little square: cross it and turn left. Follow the street nearly to the end, where the bus stop is on your left (**3h35min**).

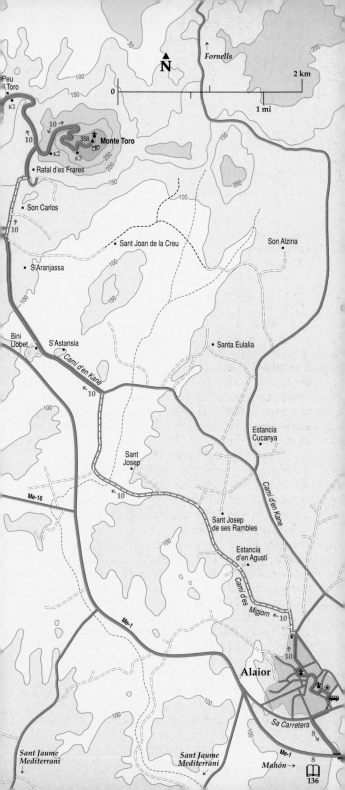

Walk 11: BESIDE THE REED BEDS: SON BOU TO SANT TOMAS

Distance: 10.4km/6.5mi; 3h30min (Note: no time has been included for exploring the caves mentioned at the very end of the walk, nor for walking to and from the bus stop to the starting point at the beach car park.)

Grade: easy

Equipment: sandals, sunhat, swimwear, towel, suncream, picnic (or have lunch in one of the many restaurants en route), plenty of water, binoculars, bird and flower recognition books

How to get there and return: 🚌 or 🚗 to/from Son Bou. Walk from the bus stop down the road to the beach and turn right. Motorists should park in the large car park to the right of the road at the rear of the beach.

Shorter walk: Sant Jaume Mediterrani. You can turn round and retrace your steps at any time after the 35min-point and pick up the walk again at the 3h15min-point.

Alternative walks

1 **Son Bou — Sant Tomàs** (5km/3mi; 1h35min; grade, equipment, access as main walk). End the walk in Sant Tomàs and take a bus or taxi back from there.

2 **Sant Tomàs — Son Bou** (5km/3mi; 1h35min; grade, equipment as main walk). Start the walk in Sant Tomàs if you are staying there, and take a taxi back from Son Bou.

3 **Son Bou, Sant Tomàs and Binigaus**. Since Walk 13 starts and finishes in Sant Tomàs, this walk can be combined with either version of that walk. For details of grade and equipment, and to estimate distance and time, see page 81.

This is a gentle, relaxing walk for naturalists (and indeed for naturists), at first along a part of the coast where in all likelihood you will see more flowers and birds than anywhere else on Menorca, and then along what are easily Menorca's longest and best beaches. It is most definitely a walk for a sunny day.

Begin at the CAR PARK at **Son Bou**: leave by the exit on the right-hand side and walk towards the sea. Do not go to the beach, but bear right and follow a little path behind the sand dunes and beside the reed beds. The marsh or LAGOON on your right is the outstanding physical feature of San Jaime/**Sant Jaume Mediterrani** and a magnet for bird life. There is nothing else like it on Menorca. All the directions you need for the next 35 minutes are: follow whichever path keeps you behind the dunes and next to the marsh; ignore any through the dunes and on to the beach.

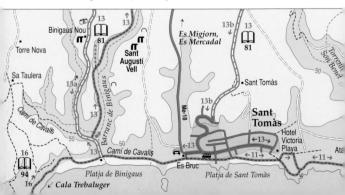

At the end of the marsh the path brings you to a GATE IN A WALL (**35min**). Beyond is tiny elevation known as **Punta Radona**, and from there a path takes you to woodland. It does not matter whether you turn left or right when you reach the wood; either fork will bring you to the holiday resort of Sant Tomàs, so I suggest you turn left on the outward leg and walk round the edge of the headland on the seaward side of the wood, then return the other way.

Beyond the headland you join the Camí de Cavalls and come to the **Platja de Sant Tomàs**, beside the HOTEL VICTORIA PLAYA (**1h05min**). You will want to explore **Sant Tomàs**, and there are three ways to cross it. Firstly you can walk along the beach; secondly you can walk behind the beach and in front of the hotels on a little promenade; thirdly you can walk along the main street. Whichever you choose, when you come to the ES BRUC RESTAURANT at the end of the Me-18 ROAD FROM ES MIGJORN (**1h35min**), turn round and make your way back.

This time, when you come to the end of Sant Tomàs beach (**2h05min**), turn left and make your way through the edge of

Lagoon and marsh at Sant Jaume Mediterrani (top and bottom); Son Bou beach (middle; Picnic 18)

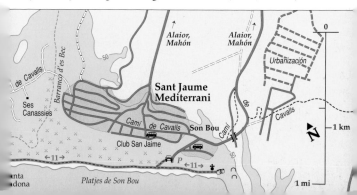

the wood beside the boundary of the hotel grounds, and turn right when you emerge. Follow the path round the outside of the wood and turn left when you reach the sea. Retrace your steps to **Punta Radona (2h35min)**. Once more you have a choice. Either go back along the marsh path or, for a change, walk back to Son Bou along the beach (or do what I do and paddle — hence the slow time for this section), stopping for a swim en route.

When you are level with the CAR PARK at **Son Bou (3h15min)**, do not stop, but carry on walking. First of all you pass a delightful picnic spot shaded by pine trees (Picnic 18) and then come to the ruins of an ancient Christian CHURCH built during the Roman Empire. Of interest is the baptismal font carved out of a single stone in the shape of a four-leaf clover. From here press on a short way for a closer look at the CAVES in the cliff ahead. Son Bou boasts one of the largest collections of prehistoric caves on the island (for more information about such caves, see the panel on page 131). Then return to the CAR PARK at **Son Bou (3h30min)**.

Flowering fields inland from Son Bou

Walk 12: THROUGH THE DEEP SOUTH

See also photographs pages 4 and 25

Distance: 12km/7.5mi; 3h

Grade: easy

Equipment: comfortable footwear, sunhat, raingear, swimwear, towel, sun-cream, picnic (or lunch at a restaurant en route), plenty of water

How to get there: 🚌 to Sant Lluís or 🚗 to Punta Prima, then 🚌 to Sant Lluís.

To return: 🚌 or 🚗 from Punta Prima

Shorter walks

1   **S'Algar — Punta Prima** (4.5km/2.8mi; 1h10min; grade, equipment, return as main walk; access: 🚌 to S'Algar). From the bus stop, walk down to the sea-front, turn right and follow the main walk from the 1h58min-point to the end.

2   **Trebalúger and Rafalet** (8km/5mi; 2h; grade, equipment as main walk; access: 🚌 or 🚗 to Sant Lluís; return: 🚌 from S'Algar). Follow the main walk to the 1h58min-point, then turn right and walk uphill to the bus stop in the centre of S'Algar; alight in Sant Lluís if you left your car there.

This is a walk of contrasting scenery. At first meandering through farming country, it later follows the coastline, visiting the delightful holiday resorts of S'Algar, Alcaufar and Punta Prima. The town of Sant Lluís was built by the French during their seven-year occupation of Menorca from 1756 to 1763. The king of France being Louis XV, the church here was dedicated by the French (Galli) to St Louis (Divo Ludovico) in 1760, as the inscription across the front proudly proclaims. Hence the name of the town. The interior of the church, though simple, is worth a visit before you start your walk. Also of interest is the windmill in the centre of town, near the bus stop, which has been converted into a museum of ethnology.

The walk begins in the little square, the **Plaça Nova**, beside the BUS STOP in the centre of **Sant Lluís**. Standing with your back to the square and facing the windmill shown on page 25, turn left and walk away from it southwards along CARRER DE SANT LLUIS. Turn down the second street on the left, CARRER DE SANT ANTONI, passing the church on your right, and follow it across a dual carriageway in the direction of Pou Nou. Ignoring several tracks to the right signposted 'Es Pou Nou', follow the country lane for 15 minutes. On your left you will see the imposing *talayot* of Trebalúger. When you come to a T-junction before the farm of RAFALETO, turn left along a walled-in track, the CAMI VELL DE TREBALUGER (**23min**), and ignore any side-turnings.

After ten minutes you will arrive at the village of **Trebalúger**, where the Camí Vell de Trebalúger becomes metalled. Two minutes later turn briefly right at a T-junction in front of a house, then almost immediately left, still on the Camí Vell de Trebalúger, ignoring streets to the right. In three minutes turn left into CAMI D'ES TALAIOT by the sign '**Talaiot de Trebalúger**', to come to the fine cyclopean building you saw earlier (**41min**). Unlike most *talayots* today, this one has steps leading up to an entrance, beyond which is a walled enclosure.

On leaving the *talayot*, retrace your steps to the Camí Vell de Trebalúger and turn right. When you come to a T-junction, turn left into CARRER DE SA TORRE. Ignore two streets on the right, then turn right into CAMI DE RAFALET. Stay on this road as it winds through the village. You will pass many side streets; ignore them. Fifteen minutes after leaving the *talayot* you will walk out of the village, passing power lines and a TRANSFORMER on your left. After three minutes ignore a track on the right leading to the farm of RAFALET PETIT but, three minutes later (just before you come to a farm building), look left: in the distance you will see a circle of military AERIAL MASTS and, between the trees, the tower of a medieval fortified farmhouse at Binissaida (seen at close quarters on Walk 6; photograph page 23). Ignore another track to the right on a bend. In three minutes the lane bends left, but straight ahead there is a gate between white pillars, and a track (**1h08min**). Go through (or, more probably, over) this gate and, soon joining the CAMI DE CAVALLS (see panel on page 100), follow the track past the lovely farmhouse of RAFALET NOU.

After 200m/yds, when you come to a gate, follow the way-marks through a gap in the wall on the right and go along a well-walked path beside a wall along the edge of a field (still on the *Camí*). Pass through another gap in a wall at the end of the field to rejoin the track and turn right. After 100m/yds the track bends to the left; leave the *Camí* here, and go through a gap in a wall on your left, down beside the **Barranc de Rafalet** (**1h24min**). The path runs through a wood of mainly holly oaks for six minutes. At the end of the path is the delightful setting for Picnic 14. On your right, in the corner, is a tiny path up which you will continue. But not before you have pressed forward to discover the minuscule **Caló d'es Rafalet**.

Return to the path and, after a short scramble, bear left at the top of the cliff. Follow one of the paths beside the creek to the end. All paths lead ultimately to the apex of the field, where a stile *(botador)* takes you over a wall to the road. Turn left and walk down the road beside the sea. At the

Entrance to the walled enclosure on the summit of the talayot *in Trebalúger*

bottom of the hill, where the road bends right, keep going straight ahead. Make your way carefully over rocky ground to the left of a wall until you reach the sea, then turn right along the promenade. At the end of the promenade (**1h58min**), keep left and walk between S'Algar Diving Centre and the sea. *(Shorter walk 1 joins here; Shorter walk 2 turns right.)* Continue between the sea on your left and a swimming pool/ restaurant on your right, towards a line of SMALL WHITE POSTS (**2h**). Go through a gap and turn right. When you come to a wall, turn left and follow a well-walked path along the coast for five minutes, to a metalled road. Turn right; it is signposted 'PLAYA/BEACH'. The road bends left to a T-junction, where you turn right. Follow this street and make your way down to the beach of **Alcaufar**.

Cross the beach and go through a gate on the far side. The Camí de Cavalls goes right here, but you follow a path to the left and uphill, ignoring paths which descend to the water's edge. The path will lead you round a headland, past tiny **Caló Roig** and, after 16 minutes, up to a WATCHTOWER (**2h 30min**). On leaving the watchtower, rejoining the *Camí* and following the path southwest along the coast for half an hour. To your left is **Illa de l'Aire**.

It was in May 1756 that Admiral John Byng had his ill-fated encounter with the French fleet in these waters. The British garrison in Fort St Philip had been besieged for two months by a French army commanded by the Duc de Richelieu that had come ashore at Ciutadella. Eighty-two year old General Blakeney waited for the Royal Navy to relieve his men. At last the garrison

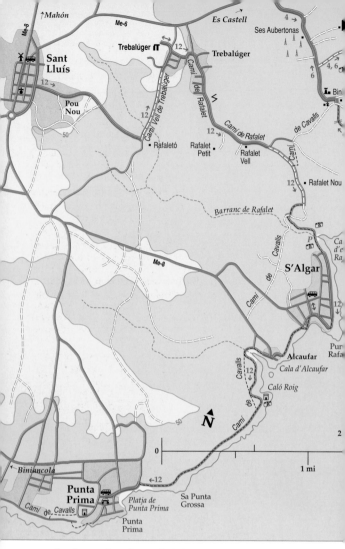

saw the fleet arrive. Out sailed the Marquis de Galissonière to engage it, but soon withdrew into Mahón harbour. Then, to the horror of the defenders, the British fleet turned about and sailed back to Gibraltar. Blakeney surrendered, and for seven years Britain was without a Mediterranean naval base. Byng was court-martialled at Portsmouth. Found guilty of negligence, he was executed by firing squad on board a captured French vessel, the Monarque, on 14th March the following year, 'pour encourager les autres,' as Voltaire wryly observed in *Candide*.

On reaching **Punta Prima**, follow the road to a left-hand bend at the end of the beach. Cross over and walk along CARRER DE XALOC (by the Hotel Xaloc) to the BUS STOP (**3h**).

WALK 13: BINIGAUS VALLEY AND COVA DES COLOMS

See also photograph page 99

Distance: 7.5km/4.7mi; 2h10min (Route a); 9.5km/6mi; 2h41min (Route b). The first 3.5km/2.2mi are common to both routes.

Grade: moderate, but with one short quite strenuous section

Equipment: walking boots (recommended after rain) or comfortable footwear, long trousers, long sleeves, sunhat, swimwear and towel, suncream, raingear, picnic (or have lunch at one of the many restaurants in Sant Tomàs at the end of the walk), plenty of water

How to get there and return: 🚌 or 🚗 to/from Sant Tomàs. Motorists should park in the car park at the end of the Me-18 road from Es Migjorn, near the Es Bruc restaurant, and join the walk at the 5min-point.

Alternative route: The route described to the Cova des Coloms is signposted and waymarked through the Barranc de Binigaus. However at times the path can be quite overgrown and narrow (hence the recommendation for long trousers and sleeves). If you find this unacceptable, retrace your steps to the 22min-point and take the wider path/track out of the clearing (it is the return path for Route a). You will climb out of the valley, pass Binigaus Nou farmhouse and, after 35 minutes, come to a gap in the wall on your right. There is a notice board here directing you along a path to the Cova des Coloms. Follow the path down into the valley bottom and on to the cave. Then join the walk as described at the 1h04min-point.

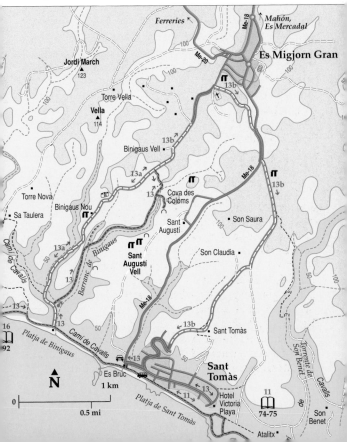

A wonderful beach, one of the best hypostyle chambers on the island, and an unbelievable cave combine to make this a very enjoyable walk. It starts in Sant Tomàs, a delightful, up-market, holiday resort on the south coast.

Begin the walk at the BUS STOP in **Sant Tomàs**. Turn to face the sea and then turn right, so that you are walking back the way the bus has just come and leaving the resort of Sant Tomàs. At the end of the street bear left and walk in front of the ES BRUC RESTAURANT and on to the BEACH (**5min**), where you join the CAMI DE CAVALLS (see page 100). Keep going in the same direction along a path above the beach for 12 minutes, at which time you will be at a large beach at the end of the **Barranc de Binigaus**. Make your way across it towards the BLOCKHOUSE shown on page 99, and turn right along a track. After three minutes you will pass through a gate and find yourself in a small clearing beside a rather fine WELL (**22min**). On your right a notice board indicates the way to the 'COVA DES COLOMS'. The way is marked with red dots and arrows. Follow a narrow path through bushes and then upwards. *(Or continue via the Alternative route, if the path is too overgrown.)*

Soon you are walking halfway up the side of the cliff, along the edge of terracing. Fifteen minutes after leaving the little clearing beside the well, you come to a CURIOUS CIRCLE OF WALLS, where the path divides. Ignore the path to the left, but bear right and go through another gap. The path will soon begin to descend again to the valley floor. After another six minutes bear left, ignoring a path to the right, and do the same again six minutes later. A couple of metres/yards further on, the path forks. Follow the left-hand waymarked path as it winds round a bush and climbs slightly before descending again to the valley floor. Nine minutes later you come to a junction with a crossing path (**1h**). Turn right and start to climb slightly, until you have crossed the valley and come to the foot of the opposite cliff. Here again notices will point you in the direction of the cave. Zigzag up the side of the cliff until you come to the entrance to the **Cova des Coloms** (**1h05min**). It is known locally as 'The Cathedral' because of its size.

When you leave the cave, walk to the other side of the valley, passing on the left the path you came by, and rise to a crossing path. Turn right to continue in the direction you were previously going. Very soon the path starts to climb quite steeply. After five minutes you pass a small flat area, where there is shade beneath a tree beside a large white rock (pleasant for a picnic). From here the path bears right and begins to climb steeply once more for another five minutes. At the top, follow the path through a gap in a wall, to emerge on a wide track (**1h18min**).

Route a: Turn left and follow this well-made track. In about 10 minutes, if you look to your left over the valley, you will see on the opposite cliff top the two *talayots* of **Sant Agustì Vell**. A further five minutes will see you before the slightly ostentatious façade of the farmhouse of BINIGAUS NOU. Climb the steps at the left of the yard and go through a gap in the wall. Cross a small yard and go through a similar gap on the opposite side. Turn left now and, in the right-hand corner, you will see steps leading down into a building that appears to have been in continuous use for one purpose or another for the last three thousand years — a beautiful example of a fairly substantial HYPOSTYLE CHAMBER (see page 13).

Make your way back to the track and turn right to carry on in the same direction as before. The track now descends into the valley and in a further 15 minutes brings you again into the little clearing by the WELL (**1h48min**; the 22min-point on your outward route). Go through the gate on your right and follow the track to the beach. Turn left, cross the end of the valley, and follow the coast back to the Es BRUC RESTAURANT (**2h05min**). Cross the road and re-enter **Sant Tomàs**, then follow the street back to the BUS STOP (**2h10min**).

Route b (There may be closures along this route; see footnote on page 84): Turn right and follow this well-made track. The farm you pass in five minutes is BINIGAUS VELL. Six minutes beyond it, ignore a track to the left, and continue ahead (now on tarmac) through a little hamlet for eight minutes, before reaching

Approaching the talayot *near Es Migjorn (Route b)*

the CEMETERY of **Es Migjorn** (**1h40min**). In a field on your left you will see a fine *talayot*. Turn right on the track just past the cemetery and follow it to the ES MIGJORN/SANT TOMAS ROAD (Me-18; **1h51min**). Cross the road, turn right and, facing the oncoming traffic, walk uphill. In four minutes, when the road reaches the top of the hill and bends right, turn left on a track (**1h55min**). Soon you will pass on your left yet another splendid *talayot*. They are reckoned to be denser in this region than anywhere else on the island. Just 400m/yds past this *talayot*, a path on the left descends to cross the Torrent de Son Benet and join the Camí de Cavalls.*

When the track divides (by a PYLON; **2h11min**), go right, beneath power lines.* In three minutes ignore the drive to SON CLAUDIA on the right; pass through some iron gates (which may or may not be open) and enter the farm of SANT TOMÀS. Walk in shade for 10 minutes, to the farmhouse. Turn right on entering the farmyard and immediately leave it via a gate on the right.* In five minutes you leave the farm and enter **Sant Tomàs** (**2h34min**). Follow the street down to a T-junction, turn right and descend quite steeply to the next T-junction. Turn right again. At the bottom of the hill turn left and cross the road, to the BUS STOP (**2h41min**). Motorists turn right here and follow the road back to the car park near the ES BRUC RESTAURANT.

*Just before press date a user reported problems south of Sant Tomàs farm. In case this track has been closed, we have added three alternatives to the map (page 81): an unblocked field track beginning 15m north of the farm, running to the centre of Sant Tomás; an alternative track (the left-hand fork) north of Son Claudia; and *(probably the safest choice)* the path via the Torrent de Son Benet, where no large farms are passed before meeting the Camí de Cavalls.

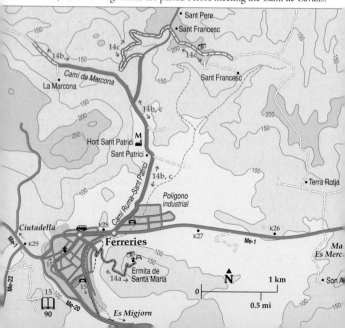

Walk 14: THREE WALKS IN THE HILLS ABOVE FERRERIES

See map opposite; also photographs on pages 2, 11

Walk a: Ermita de Santa Maria (3.2km/2mi; 50min; moderate)

Walk b: La Marcona (6km/3.7mi; 1h30min; easy)

Walk c: Sant Francesc (7.5km/4.6mi; 1h52min; strenuous)

Equipment: walking boots (Walk a) or comfortable footwear, sunhat, suncream, raingear, binoculars, picnic, plenty of water

How to get there and return: 🚌 or 🚗 to/from Ferreries. Motorists should park where convenient — by the football ground for Walk a, or at the edge of the industrial estate for Walks b and c.

A pproaching Ferreries from the east, you cannot fail to notice the brightly coloured tower of a little chapel perched on top of a hill overlooking the town. Walk a takes you up to that chapel, from where you will have splendid views over the town and surrounding countryside. Walk b may well be the quietest walk you will do — apart from time spent in the cheese factory. Make sure you do it in the morning, when the cheese factory is open. Walk c runs partly along the ridge to the north of Ferreries, affording splendid views over the northern beaches of Pregonda and Binimel-là.

Begin Walk a at the RESTAURANT beside the BUS STOP in **Ferreries**. Walk along the street to the left of the restaurant. It is CARRER DE SON GRANOT, but you will not see the name until you are halfway along it. Cross AVINGUDA DE SON MORERA and a STORM DRAIN, and keep straight ahead. At the end of this street, climb a flight of steps.* At the top, follow a narrow path to the right; then, after about 20m/yds, turn left on a wider, crossing path. This is an old pilgrims' trail to the little church of St Mary on the hilltop. Look out for the 'stations' — large stones inscribed with the titles of the Virgin Mary. When you meet another crossing path/track (**4min**) turn right and follow it as it winds up for 15 minutes, to a little gem of a church, the **Ermita de Santa Maria (25min)**. Only the tiny sanctuary is completely enclosed, the body of the church has only low walls and no roof. Two stone benches along the rear wall provide the only seating. Behind the church, beyond a small building, there is perhaps the prettiest shady picnic spot on the whole island, with stone table and benches.

Begin your descent now to return to the town. After 15 minutes turn left and, four minutes later, turn right down the little path that takes you to the flight of steps. Walk straight ahead along CARRER DE SON GRANOT, to the BUS STOP (**50min**).

Start Walk b by walking away from the BUS STOP along the

---

*At time of writing, roadworks were in progress here; the route may change. There should be a sign indicating the *ermita* via one of the paths on the map.

Me-1 main road in the direction of Es Mercadal. At the round-about, turn left and walk to the left of the industrial estate (*Polìgono industrial;* motorists should park here). Beyond the estate the wide road turns into a pleasant country lane. After 15 minutes you will arrive at the magnificent HORT SANT PATRICI cheese factory. It is open for visits morning and evening every day except Sunday. There are cheese tastings and a musum.

When you leave the cheese factory, carry on in the same direction for another five minutes, to where the road forks (**25min**). Turn left along the CAMÍ DE LA MARCONA. The road undulates through quiet and lovely countryside for 13 minutes,

Above: approaching the Ermita de Santa Maria (Walk 14a) and (left) the lovely picnic spot behind the little church

before bringing you to the entrance to LA MARCONA farm, where the tarmac stops. Although the track continues ahead for some distance, after seven minutes the way is barred by a PADLOCKED GATE, so turn round at that point and retrace your steps to the fork (**1h05min**).

Turn right (or, for a longer walk, turn left and follow the directions for Walk c from the 25min-point) and walk back past the cheese factory and industrial estate. Turn right at the roundabout on the Me-1 and return to the BUS STOP (**1h30min**).

To start Walk c follow the directions for Walk b as far as the 25min-point. Then bear right. After about 550m/yds, turn off left on a meandering track which climbs ever more steeply for 25 minutes, until you reach the lane you left earlier, beside the farm of SANT FRANCESC. Cross the road and continue on another track. To your left there are two farms, SANT FRANCESC immediately to your left, and beyond it SANT PERE. Both have pictures of the saint they are named for over the door: Saint Francis and Saint Peter.

As you follow the track you will now have good views over the island to the northern and southern beaches, as well as the gardens of HORT SANT PATRICI. Pass through a gateway marked 'SON GRANGES' but, when you come to the entrance to a second Sant Francesc, bear left over a cattle grid.

Eleven minutes after reaching the top of the hill, you will come to a LOCKED GATE (**1h01min**), where once more you must turn round and retrace your steps. You will reach the CAMI DE LA MARCONA fork in 26 minutes. Carry on past the CHEESE FACTORY and INDUSTRIAL ESTATE. Turn right at the roundabout on the Me-1 and return to the BUS STOP (**1h52min**).

Walk 15: THE GORGES AND PREHISTORIC VILLAGE OF SON MERCER

Distance: 13.3km/8.3mi; 3h35min

Grade: strenuous, with an overall ascent/descent of 140m/460ft

Equipment: walking boots or comfortable shoes or trainers, sunhat, raingear, suncream, long trousers, picnic, plenty of water

How to get there and return: 🚌 or 🚗 to/from Ferreries (park beside the main road or by the football ground in Carrer Formentera).

Shorter walks (grade, equipment, access as above)

1   **Barranc de Sa Cova** (10.5km/6.5mi; 2h57min). Follow the main walk to the 1h55min-point, turn right, and follow the notes from the 2h33min-point.

2   **Prehistoric village** (11km/6.8mi; 2h41min). Follow the main walk to the 41min-point but, instead of turning left, keep straight ahead towards a farm building. Go through a gate and carry on until you reach Son Mercer de Baix. Cross the farmyard, and in three minutes, when you meet a track coming from the left, keep straight ahead and pick up the notes at the 1h55min-point.

The farms of Son Mercer are situated on a small plateau entirely surrounded by precipitous cliffs and deep gorges, the *barrancs* of Trebalúger and Sa Cova, and the *torrent* of Son

The Bronze Age settlement at Son Mercer de Baix is the best place on the island to view some of the deep valleys that gouge their way to the sea across southern Menorca. In this photograph the Barranc de Sa Cova leads the eye to Monte Toro (Walk 10) in the distance.

Gras. Such terrain is ideal for bird life. And also for defence. It was here, in one of the most unassailable positions on the island, that a group of talayotic people decided to build their village; the views they enjoyed are breathtaking, as you can see in the photograph opposite. Incidentally, the farms' name illustrates perfectly the multiplicity of Menorquín spellings. There are no less than four versions — Mercé, Marcé, Marcer, Mercer. I have chosen the last because it is on the farm gate.

Start the walk at the RESTAURANT beside the BUS STOP in **Ferreries**. Walk along the street to the left of the restaurant (CARRER DE SON GRANOT). Ahead you will see a hill with a small chapel on top. At the second crossroads, turn right along AVINGUDA DE SON MORERA, with a concrete STORM DRAIN on your left. Follow this tree-lined avenue past the FOOTBALL GROUND (where motorists could park). At the end of the trees, head diagonally right for some 80m/yds*, to emerge at a T-junction (the MAIN ME-20 ROAD; **11min**). Turn left towards Es Migjorn.

Six minutes after crossing the river bridge, turn right. Go over a cattle grid and begin to climb up a concrete track. A notice by the cattle grid states that the *poblat* is only open on Saturdays. This is to keep cars from clogging the farm tracks during the working week. It does not prevent you from walking there. Nor should you (on foot) have any problem accessing the site. You will however have to climb over the occasional gate, locked to bar the way for cars. In three minutes ignore a track on the left, and in a further 12 minutes, after passing some fine MEGALITHS at the

*There were road/buildings works here at time of writing. Possibly Son Morera will be extended all the way to the Me-20

SOME ANCIENT CUSTOMS

Besides telling of their skill with the sling, the writers of antiquity have left us other fascinating glimpses of the inhabitants of prehistoric villages like the one on this walk. For example, one name for the islands was 'the Gymnasiae', given (according to one writer) 'because the inhabitants go about naked during the summer'. *Plus ça change* … only perhaps we should change 'inhabitants' to 'visitors'. But if that is the case, we must hope that it does not apply equally to another of their customs: 'At the wedding the bride was first possessed by the friends and relations of the bridegroom in exchange for gifts'. One thing the writers all agree on — the warriors wore no armour in battle. In fact they had little time for metal. There was a ban on the import and use of gold and silver, of which none has been found by archaeologists, and the victorious warrior much preferred to take his spoil in women and wine. In fact they prized women highly, and if their women were carried off by enemies, they would make every effort to ransom them. Lacking gold, they would give three or four men of rank in exchange.

side of the road, you will arrive at the farm of SON MERCER DE DALT.

Turn right, and then keep straight ahead through a gateway, along a well-made but unsealed road, with farm buildings to your left and a lovely farmhouse on your right. In five minutes, having passed a slurry pit and gone through another gateway, ignore a track on the right. Some 100m/yds further on, turn left down a broad track (**41min**). *(But for Shorter walk 2, keep straight ahead.)* Eight minutes later the track turns right, through a gateway, and narrows. In four minutes go through another gateway. Some 100m/yds further on, climb over a third iron gate; ahead is the valley of the **Torrent de Son Gras**. Descend now to the valley floor (**1h08min**).

Pass through a gap in a wall, into a large field. Early in the summer, if it is in crop, walk along the right-hand edge (but watch out for brambles). When the crop has been harvested it is easier. At the end you exit through a gap into a short, walled-in track. Turn left and walk down the track. Turn right at the end and go through a gate on your right into a large cherry ORCHARD. Cross the orchard, walking along the right-hand boundary, and go up steps past an outbuilding. Go through a gate and turn left. Carry on along a good track above and to the right of the orchard (**1h22min**). If you should ever have trouble leaving the cherry orchard by this gate, carry on walking along the right-hand edge of the field for 100m/yds, where another gate will allow you access to the track.

You now climb back out of the valley, above the **Barranc de Sa Cova**. After some 20 minutes go through a gate (**1h44min**). All the gateways between this point and the junction at 1h55min are cattle grids with wooden gates beside them. Turn right at another one in 50m/yds, to cross a wide field. When, in three

This important junction is passed twice during the walk: at 1h55min and at 2h33min. The flat countryside beyond the typical Menorcan wooden gate is deceptive. Between the cowshed and the distant farms deep, steep-sided valleys cut through the landscape.

minutes, you pass another gate, you will see the farm of Son Mercer de Baix ahead. You pass two more gates, in three and eight minutes, and go by the shed seen in the photograph above, before coming to an important junction (**1h55min**), where the farm is to the right. Turn left on a walled-in track. *(Shorter walk 1 turns right here; Shorter walk 2 comes in here and keeps straight ahead.)*

You might check your watch now, as it is easy to miss the entrance to the site — it's 15 to 20 minutes from here (just over 1km). After the prehistoric village the track starts to descend, so if you find yourself going *downhill*, you have gone too far. The PREHISTORIC VILLAGE (**2h15min**) lies to your left, beyond a gate; there is a site plan and information in English and German as well as the two local languages. Most of the buildings are little more than foundations, but there is one hypostyle chamber that is more intact, with three pillars, typically wider at the top than the bottom, supporting the roof. For the best views, walk up to the rear of the village and look out eastwards over the Barranc de Sa Cova (photograph page 88).

When you leave the village, retrace your steps past the track you climbed from the valley (**2h33min**), and cross the SON MERCER DE BAIX farmyard. In seven minutes go through a gate, and eight minutes later another. Pass some farm buildings on the left and then the track you took to descend into the valley (**2h53min**). Go by SON MERCER DE DALT and the MEGALITHS, and descend the twisting track back to the MAIN ME-20 ROAD (**3h10min**) at **Ferreries**. Turn left. Pass your outward route and fork right on CARRER DE MIGJORN GRAN. Pass the FOOTBALL GROUND and fork right to cross the little **Plaça Menorca** and continue along CARRER PAU PONS. This brings you into the main square, the **Plaça Espanya**, where you turn right to follow the AVINGUDA VERGE DEL TORO back to the BUS STOP (**3h35min**).

Walk 16: CALA MITJANA AND TREBALUGER BAY (WITH AN OPTIONAL EXTENSION TO SANT TOMÀS)

See map pages 96-97; see also photographs pages 29, 98

Distance: 8.5km/5.3mi; 2h46min

Grade: The entire route is very well signed with waymarking posts — at first along the Camí de Cavalls. The section between Cala Santa Galdana and Cala Mitjana is easy. The section between Cala Mitjana and Trebalúger Bay has some short but quite difficult climbs and descents and requires some agility. It is *not recommended for small children, the elderly or infirm.*

Equipment: walking boots (for the section between Cala Mitjana and Trebalúger Bay) or comfortable footwear, sunhat, raingear, suncream, picnic, plenty of water, swimwear, towel, binoculars

How to get there and return: 🚌 or 🚗 to/from Cala Santa Galdana. Travelling by bus, it may be necessary to go to Ferreries first. By car, at the roundabout at the entrance to the resort, take the middle road and turn right over the bridge. Park in the large car park on the right.

Short walk: Cala Santa Galdana to Cala Mitjana (5km/3mi; 1h30min; grade: easy; equipment as above, but comfortable footwear will suffice) Since this is a out-and-back walk, you can stop at Cala Mitjana by jumping from the 44min- point to the 2h point and continuing the walk from there.

Extension: from Cala Santa Galdana to Sant Tomàs (10km/6.2mi; 3h10min; grade and equipment as main walk *beyond Cala Mitjana:* this is strenuous walking — the ups and downs on the whole stretch are around 250m/1000ft). 🚌 to Cala Santa Galdana to start; return by 🚌 from Sant Tomàs. See the map and notes on page 94 to complete this wonderful extension to the outward route of the main walk described below.

Perhaps because it is one of its loveliest bays, Cala Trebalúger is one of Menorca's most closely-guarded secrets. As beautiful as the beach is the valley behind it, where the gorges seen on Walk 15 finally meet the sea.

Begin by leaving the BUS STOP/CAR PARK in **Cala Santa Galdana** and making your way to the BEACH. Facing the sea, turn left and cross to the far side where you will find a flight of steps. Climb to the top of the cliff, and in 20m/yds turn left along the road. In under 150m/yds you will reach a car parking area. Turn right along a short street here, joining the CAMÍ DE CAVALLS (**20min**; see panel on page 100). Beyond the turning circle continue along a short track through a wall. After 20m/yds the path divides. Fork left in the direction of houses and a stone wall.

Ten minutes after turning into the Camí de Cavalls the path runs through a gateway and takes you to a track. Turn right, and after 150m/yds, turn right again and go through a gateway beside notice boards. Ignoring a path to the right and then two to the left, follow this wide track downhill until you reach the sea at **Cala Mitjaneta** (photograph page 29). On your left are more notice boards. These explain the working of a former LIMESTONE QUARRY which lies at the end of a short path to the left.

Continue to follow the track for eight minutes, until you

92

MARITIME ZONE MARKERS

From the high water mark for six metres inland, all the coastline of Spain belongs to the state, and along this strip the walker has right of access (unless it has been appropriated by the military). The boundary of this maritime zone is indicated by small concrete markers inscribed 'ZMT'. You will see these markers on all the coastal walks in this book.

Photograph: Cala Trebalúger

come to steps going down to **Cala Mitjana** (**45min**; Picnic 10). Behind the *cala* is a large car park with picnic tables. (The Camí de Cavalls heads off from the northeast corner of the car park, running inland via the Barranc de Trebalúger. It doesn't come back to the coast until the Platja de Binigaus. *Walkers* may wonder why, since a perfectly well waymarked coastal path already exists, the *Camí* has been routed inland along this stretch. Probably the answer is that the path from here to Binigaus would not be 'safe for travellers on *horseback*'. But do not be astonished to encounter macho mountain bikers on the path — even on the strenuous extension described overleaf.)

Head straight across the beach, towards a MARITIME ZONE MARKER similar to the one shown above, and climb on to the ledge. Turn right and follow the path up a narrow waymarked path to the top of the cliff. Five minutes should see you at the top, where the path leads you to a drystone wall. Bear slightly left and follow the path into a wood — only before you do so, take time to walk to your right, to a viewpoint overlooking the lovely *cala* you have just left. After walking into the wood for about 100m/yds, ignore a track to the left and keep ahead on the well-worn path. In seven minutes ignore a track on the right, and turn left. Two minutes later fork left, pass a LIMEKILN, and after 15m/yds turn right (**1h04min**).

The path cuts through two walls, and in four minutes emerges from the wood into a field. Walk beside the bushes on your right

93

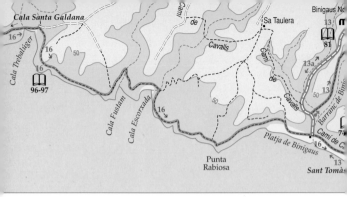

to the far side of the field and re-enter woodland. Go through a gap in a wall, and then, slowly at first, begin to descend. The last ten minutes of descent, mostly on cut steps, are quite steep — take care: the drop from the last step down into the narrow river is about 1m/3ft and requires agility. You may have to paddle across the end of the stream to reach the sand of a glorious bay, **Cala Trebalúger (1h25min)**.

It is unlikely to be deserted; not only is it visited by boats bringing holidaymakers for a barbecue lunch, but since the opening and waymarking of the through route to Sant Tomàs this hitherto infrequently visited stretch of coast will see many more walkers. But you should find plenty of open space shaded by pine trees, where you can picnic. Before leaving the beach, walk away from the sea and through the wood, to look out over the river at the end of the valley. Not only is the view most attractive but, if you are lucky, you may also see one of Menorca's most attractive birds, the bee-eater, which nests here. If not, you should at least see a heron as some kind of consolation.

If you are walking back to Cala Santa Galdana, retrace your outgoing route. Landfalls on the way back are the LIMEKILN (**1h44min**), **Cala Mitjana (2h)**, the CAMI DE CAVALLS (**2h26min**) and **Cala Santa Galdana**, where you make your way towards the far side of the bay, cross the river bridge, and turn right, back to the BUS STOP/CAR PARK (**2h46min**).

Extension: If you are carrying on to Sant Tomàs, be prepared for many more ups and downs, but all the potentially vertiginous drops are well protected. There are plenty of waymarker posts. Landfalls en route are **Cala Fustam (35 min;** this beach could compete with Cala Sa Torreta for seaweed!), **Cala Excorxada (55min)**, and **Punta Rabiosa (1h10min)**. Eventually you come to the BLOCKHOUSE shown on page 99 (**1h28min**). This is where Walk 13 turns up into the **Barranc de Binigaus**. From here it's under 20 minutes' walking — mostly along the beach — to the BUS STOP at **Sant Tomàs (1h45min; 3h10min** from Cala Santa Galdana). See the map on page 81 if in doubt about the route.

Walk 17: CALA SANTA GALDANA • TORRE TRENCADA • CALA MACARELLA • CALA SANTA GALDANA

See also cover photograph

Distance: 20.5km/12.7mi; 5h30min

Grade: moderate

Equipment: comfortable footwear, sunhat, raingear, suncream, picnic, plenty of water, swimwear, towel

How to get there and return: 🚌 or 🚗 to/from Cala Santa Galdana. By car, at the roundabout at the entrance to the resort, take the middle road and turn right over the bridge. Park in the large car park on the right.

Shorter walk: Barranc d'Algendar (6km/3.8mi; 1h20min; quite easy; equipment, access as main walk). Follow the main walk to the 13min-point. Turn right here, and carry on along the valley floor. After seven minutes, ignore a path to the right crossing the valley and, on coming to a second gate, climb over the wall at the side of it. Six minutes later the route forks round a large bush (although you may not even see this fork) — your way is to the right, through a field. Another 17 minutes' walking will bring you to a wonderful outlook over the Barranc d'Algendar. A reinforced mesh fence blocks further progress, so from here retrace your route to the car park in Cala Santa Galdana.

Alternative walk: Cala Santa Galdana to Ferreries (15km/9.3mi; 3h; grade, equipment and access by 🚌 as main walk; return on 🚌 from Ferreries). At the 1h52min-point in the main walk, you join the cycle route between Ciutadella and Ferreries. Follow this to the right. It runs through the gorge of the Algendar *barranc* and comes onto the Me-1 in Ferreries 80m/yds north of the junction with the Me-20. Although there is no map for the latter part of this walk, you can use the map overleaf to begin and the map on page 90 to make your way through Ferreries.

Walk up the *barranc* of Algendar while the birds are singing, have lunch around a megalithic table in a Bronze Age village, enjoy the beauty of Macarella's valley, refresh yourselves on its beach, and finally walk beneath pines back to Cala Santa Galdana.

Start the walk at the BUS STOP/CAR PARK at **Cala Santa Galdana**: turn right and walk away from the sea. Walk beside the **Algendar** River into the valley. Beyond a splendid palm tree the metalled road becomes a gravel track. Ten minutes into the walk you reach a gate. Three minutes later the track divides (**13min**). Take the rising track on the left. After about 15 minutes you pass the entrance to SON MESTRES farm on the left and in another 25 minutes or so come to the SANTA GALDANA farm buildings (**55min**).

Curl right, then left, past the farm, keeping the farmhouse on your right, passing a cowshed on your left, and going beneath power lines. At the end of the farm drive climb a stile over another gate and turn right on a metalled country lane. There will be little traffic because it leads nowhere. In eight minutes, when the lane turns left, you will see on the hill in front the three farms of TORRE

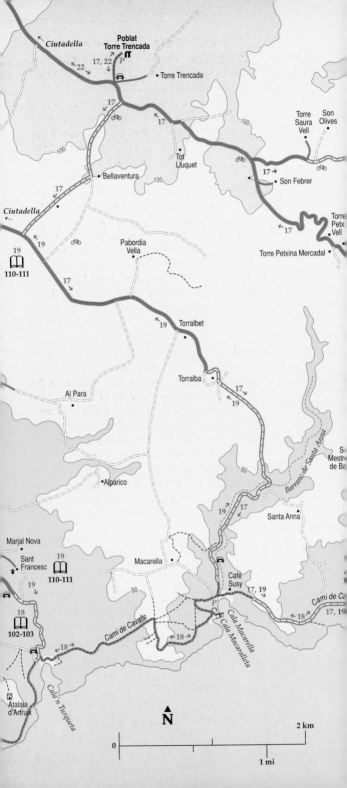

Ciutadella

22

17, 22

Poblat Torre Trencada

P ⁝⁝

Torre Trencada

17

17

Torre Saura Vell

Son Olives

100

Tot Lluquet

17 →

Son Febrer

Bellaventura

100

Torre Petx Vell

17

Ciutadella ←

17

19

Torre Petxina Mercadal ·

19

📖 110-111

Pabordia Vella

17

19 → Torralbet

Al Para

Torralba

17 →

19

Barranc de Santa Anna

S· Mestre de Ba·

50

·Alparico

19 → 17

Santa Anna

Marjal Nova

Sant Francesc

19 📖 110-111

Macarella

Café Susy

17, 19

Cami de Ca·

19

18 →

17, 19

18 📖 102-103

Cami de Cavalls

18 →

Cala Macarella

Cala Macarelleta

50

18 →

18 →

Atalaia d'Artruix

Cala 'n Turqueta

N

0   1 mi   2 km

PETXINA: Nou, Vell, and Mercadal. As you walk up to the farms, the hill to your right is (appropriately enough) Torre Petxina (115m/380ft).

Beyond the farms you cross a valley, and climb to pass Torre Petxina SCHOOL and the entrance to SON FEBRER farm (**1h53min**). In four minutes, as you pass under power lines, ignore a road on the right; it's part of the Ciutadella/Ferreries cycle route. *(But turn right here for the Alternative walk to Ferreries.)* The main walk follows the cycle route to the left. You will pass the entrance to TOT LLUQUET farm in 13 minutes, and nine minutes later a gated track on the left (**2h19min**) — part of the cycle route to Ciutadella. You will be returning along this track after visiting the prehistoric settlement ahead. Two minutes later you will be in the little parking area provided for visitors to the site, from where a signposted path leads across the fields to the prehistoric settlement of **Torre Trencada** (**2h29min**; Picnic 13).

To continue the walk, return to the car park and turn left. Ignore the road on the left to Torre Trencada farm, and walk straight ahead until you come to the track you saw earlier. Turn right along this track. It is barred to motorised traffic — otherwise it would make a handy short-cut for cars from the Ferreries/Ciutadella highway to the southern beaches, enabling them to avoid Ciutadella.

In nine minutes pass farm buildings, and four minutes later follow the track to the right, leaving Bellaventura farm (and the cycle route) to your left. You pass one more house on your left before reaching a tarmac road (**3h10min**). (Walk 19 follows this road west to Sant Joan de Missa.) Turn left here. Having passed the drives to BELLAVENTURA and PABORDIA VELLA farms, you will come to the farm of TORRALBET in **3h35min**.

Keep on the road for seven minutes, until the asphalt stops and the way forks. Take the track to the left signed 'MACARELLA', which bypasses the farm of TORRALBA. Go through a gate, over a cattle grid, and keep straight ahead. In 10 minutes the track

starts to descend quite steeply into the valley. It is wooded and shaded now, spoiled only by the dust thrown up by cars making for the beach. A little over half an hour past Torralba farm you arrive at **Cala Macarella (4h 20min**; Picnic 11). Walks 18 and 19 also visit this beach. You will be grateful now for CAFETERIA SUSY by the beach, with toilets and showers, where you can refresh yourselves.

To continue, join the well-waymarked CAMÍ DE CAVALLS (see page 100) and begin the steep ascent of a splendid wooden staircase with no less

Cala Santa Galdana: Menorcans regard it as their most beautiful beach and bitterly regret its 'urbanización'. There is no saint named Galdana; the name is a corruption of the Moorish 'Guad-al-Ana' (barranc of St Anne'), after whom the adjacent farm is named. Car tour 2 and Walks 16-18 visit this cove.

than 214 steps. Bear left at the top along a wide path. After about 15 minutes the route forks. Turn left, clambering down over rocks, keeping beside a wall on your left as you have done since the path reached the top of the cliff. Two minutes later do something similar (there are waymarks, and you may spot a red dot on a stone as well). During the next eight minutes ignore occasional paths to the right, and continue to follow the wide track beside the wall (photograph below). You will come to a wall with two gaps in it. Choose the higher one, on the left. Go through it, and turn left along a narrow path (**4h50min**). In 20m/yds turn right along a good track. Walk through a pine wood for seven minutes (past a short-cut path) until you come to a T-junction where you turn right. In six minutes turn right when the track forks, and six minutes later you will pass through a gate. Now **Cala Santa Galdana** lies before you (**5h10min**). Turn left and follow the road round to the right. Almost at once go down steps on your right, and go down to the bay past the HOTEL AUDAX. Turn left once more, and walk round the bay to the CAR PARK/BUS STOP (**5h30min**).

BLOCKHOUSES

Every beach on Menorca where enemy forces could possibly be landed is guarded with tiny blockhouses of varying dates. Some date from the 18th century, when France and Britain fought over the island, for at that time Mahón harbour was Britain's equivalent of America's Pearl Harbour. These blockhouses have a dozen or so small apertures for musketeers/ riflemen, and are built of stone.

Others date from the Spanish Civil War (1936-9); the small, concrete structures with only one or two openings are machine-gun posts. Some are almost intact, sometimes providing accommodation for bats, others have crumbled away, whilst a few, like so many other ancient buildings here, provide free holiday homes.

Above: blockhouse at Binigaus (Walk 13); below: In October the track from Cala Santa Galdana to Cala Macarella is brightened by autumn crocuses.

CAMI DE CAVALLS

Consequent on the blockhouses (see page 99) and watchtowers (page 107) was the need to be able to get soldiers to and from them. So from early times there existed a road more or less following the perimeter of the island. It is mentioned in literature dating from the 16th century, and came into prominence during the time of the British and French occupations of the 18th century.

In fact archives in Mahón record that the first British lieutenant-governor, Sir Richard Kane, ordered the 'old King's Road around the coast to be marked out in March of every year with closely-spaced fresh green branches, the cost of this work to be born by the landowners through whose territory the road passes'. Moreover, 'where the road runs some distance inland, it should be re-routed closer to the coast — provided that the new route would be safe for travellers on horseback'. This coastal road is known in Catalan as the 'Camí de Cavalls' (bridle-road). It was last used during the Spanish Civil War (1936-9), when the Republicans ordered it to be cleared ready for use, with all landowners' obstructions removed. But at the end of the war it fell into disuse and became so overgrown that in places it could not

even be identified. Other parts fell under tarmac through housing developments. But one of the major obstacles for those who tried to follow the *Camí* were the many obstacles put in their way by land-owners — as users of this guide have found to their cost!

In the late 90s a group of Menorcans formed a society to 'defend' the *Camí*. This pressure group succeeded in having an act passed by the Balearic Parliament in 2000 guaranteeing the reinstatement of the road for the benefit of walkers, cyclists and riders. It took eight years to dot the 'i's and cross the 't's, but the *Camí* is now freely accessible — *where it has been cleared.* Work is still going on along some stretches, so

don't expect perfect waymarking throughout. Sections that are finished are usually indicated by a wooden post with a 'horseshoe' plaque. This of course opens up many more opportunities for walks than those described in this book. The whole trail is 179km long; the touring map shows the route and the 'official' starting points (broken down into 15 segments). You should be able to get more information from the nearest tourist office (and a booklet of 20 suggested routes has just been published).

Reports suggest that — *in places where the work has been completed* — it's very easily followed.

Photograph: Camí de Cavalls above the Cala de Sant Esteve (Walk 6)

Walk 18: A COASTAL WALK BETWEEN CALA'N BOSCH AND CALA SANTA GALDANA

See also photograph on page 98

Maps on pages 96-97 and overleaf

Grade: moderate

Equipment: comfortable footwear, sunhat, raingear, suncream, picnic, plenty of water, swimwear, towel

Distance, How to get there and return: See below and page 105.

Shorter walk: Son Saura — Cala'n Turqueta — Son Saura (6.5km/4mi; 1h50min; grade: easy; equipment as above) 🚗: See Picnic 20 on page 19 to drive to Son Saura beach. Then pick up the Cala'n Bosch to Cala Santa Galdana walk below at the 1h40min-point and follow it as far as Cala'n Turqueta (the 2h37min-point). Now turn to the 1h36min-point of the Cala Santa Galdana to Cala'n Bosch walk (page 106) and retrace your steps back to Platja de Son Saura.

Sometimes winding through beautiful countryside, sometimes beside the sea, continually descending to breath-taking beaches, often following ancient tracks and passing ancient buildings, this walk — which follows the Camí de Cavalls (see opposite) throughout, may well prove to be many people's favourite. It is described fully in both directions. Since it is a long walk, you may wish to follow only part of it and then retrace your steps. (To make this easier, at each time check I have inserted, *in italics,* the time check if walking in the reverse direction.)

From Cala'n Bosch to Cala Santa Galdana

Distance: 16km/10mi; 4h22min

How to get there: 🚌 to Cala'n Bosch (alight at the Cala'n Bosch Hotel). Or 🚗 (only possible if you intend to walk part way, and then to retrace your steps to Cala'n Bosch). Drive to Cala'n Bosch. Follow the Me-24 nearly to the lighthouse at Cap d'Artruix and turn left. Drive by the sea and follow the road round to the left, where you will see a footbridge over the entrance to the marina. Park near the bridge, and walk over it to the Cala'n Bosch Hotel, to begin the walk.

To return: 🚌 from Cala Santa Galdana or 🚗 from Cala'n Bosch

Begin the walk by heading across the beach of **Cala'n Bosch** and climbing up to the headland on the far side. Walk round the headland on a well-trodden path and you will arrive at a car park. Walk across to the adjacent bay, **Son Xoriguer,** and follow the promenade to the far side. Carry on until you are nearly at the opposite HEADLAND (**20min**) *(4h07min)*. Look now for a sandy track going away to the left, part of the Camí de Cavalls mentioned opposite. Turn along that track, soon skirting a dry-stone wall. The sea is never far away to your right, as the way takes you between bushes. After 0.5km/0.3mi a similar track goes off left, but ignore that, and continue to walk parallel with the sea. In 100m/yds you will come to a wall that goes down to the sea. Go through a gateway and shortly you will reach **Cala**

101

Parejals. This is a forbidding place, much eroded by the sea and giving the impression that the whole cliff is about to collapse. It is watched over by a machine-gun post, the first of many military buildings and blockhouses along this coast. Notice the steps by a little white building which lead to a mooring in a cave below. The building houses the machinery for raising a boat out of the water. Beyond this building fork right; the left fork leads to So Na Parets Nous farm. After 200m/yds go through a wooden gate (**45min**) (*3h42min*).

Continue with a wall to your left and **Punta Prima** to your right. In six minutes go through a gap in a wall, ignore a path to the left, and walk across rocky ground towards bushes opposite. The *Camí* winds round the next seaweedy bay, **Cala de Son Vell**. Follow it round the back of bushes and start to go down to the little bay. Before you get there, turn left round a squatters' camp and go up an ancient track. The bedrock surface of this cart-track is deeply worn and rutted in places, testifying both to its antiquity and the volume of traffic which once made its way to this isolated bay in an age when the sea offered the easiest way of moving about the island. You pass a curious megalithic enclosure on the left and, in 100m/yds, arrive at a T-junction. Turn right here and follow the track for another 350m/yds until, 50m/yds before it reaches a wall, you turn right along a path which brings you to a gate lower down in the wall (**1h01min**) (*3h22min*).

Beyond the gate, follow the path ahead, veering towards the sea. In a couple of minutes you pass between a pair of CAVES. The one on the right is worth exploring, since it is a good example of a Menorcan troglodyte home. The central pillar giving support to the roof, and the pilaster on the right, are common features.

The path continues eastwards until reaching shrubby terrain. Pass between bushes on the left and the **Pesquera d'es Conde** on the seaward side. Cross the end of a headland, beyond which is a little *cala*. Continue round the beach, past two BLOCKHOUSES. In 200m/yds you will arrive at the **Racó d'es Pi**, with the beach of Son Saura in view. If you look straight across the bay, you will see another military post on a hilltop — the medieval

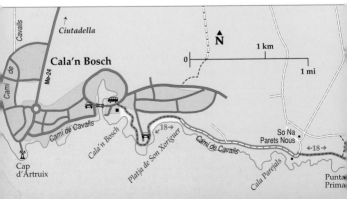

WATCHTOWER OF **Artruix**, shown on page 107. The path descends to sea level, crossing a slipway and passing another gun post. Here you join another ancient cart track. When you come to a wall, go through a gate and walk onto the beach of **Platja de Son Saura** (1h40min) *(2h37min)*. *(The Shorter walk joins here.)*

Walk round the first half of the bay, then cross the little rock outcrop that bisects the bay. Follow the path to a bridge over a drain and walk round the second half of the bay. Some 200m/yds before the end, ignore the path to the left, crossing the headland. Follow the *Camí* along the cliffs and down to **Cala d'es Talaier**, just about perfect for your picnic (2h) *(2h21min)*. If you bear left and follow a path round the back of trees at the rear of the beach it will bring you to the end of the *cala*. Begin to walk towards the beach, but soon bear left towards wooden poles barring access. Just to the right of them, climb a narrow path through trees. Soon you come to a wall and turn right. On your left you will see the tower shown in the photograph on page 107. After 10 minutes turn right along a narrow path. This brings you close to the sea, with lovely views. In 11 minutes ignore a path to the left, and 50m/yds after that you will be beside the wall again. Walk beside the wall for no more than 50m/yds, then turn right down a little path between bushes. Keep following the waymarked path towards Turqueta Beach. About eight minutes after turning down this little path you will come to a T-junction. Turn right, still heading down to the beach, and in 50m/yds turn left down steps. Clamber up the other side, go over a wall and through what appear to be the remains of a former building. Beyond it turn left, away from the sea, until you come to a similar gateway to the one you met at Talaier. Go through it and turn left. Walk beside a wall, shortly ignoring a turning through it, then descend through trees. At the bottom is a wall which borders a car park. Turn left, then sharply right at the end of the wall and go through the car park and on to the beach of **Cala'n Turqueta** (2h44min) *(1h36min)*. *(The Shorter walk returns from here.)*

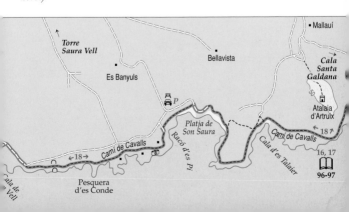

To continue the walk, pass the toilets beyond the car park and bear left to climb up a sandy path. For a few minutes you climb through a pine wood, before emerging into more open country. Now the path bends left; ignore a path on the right. For five minutes the path winds through low bushes before reaching a wall. Pass through a gateway. Keep straight ahead now, with a wall on your left. After another seven minutes the path has widened and brought you to a major junction, where you turn right (**3h06min**) *(1h13min)*. Shortly, ignore a path off left and two paths on the right, and descend through a small valley that bring you to another superb little beach, **Cala Macarelleta** (**3h16min**) *(56min)*.

Cross to the left-hand side of the beach (as you face the sea),

Cala Macarelleta

then take the steps cut into the rock, which turn left and wind their way up to the top of the cliff. From the top of the steps a short path leads to a T-junction with a broad path. Your way is left, but before leaving, walk in the opposite direction to the END OF THE HEADLAND, where you have splendid views over both Macarelleta beach and its larger neighbour, Macarella.

Retrace your steps and pass the short path. Two minutes later, when the path turns right, ignore a path on the left, and in 50m/yds turn right down a rocky path. Go through a gap in a wall, and keep descending until you emerge at the rear of **Cala Macarella (3h34min)** *(40min)*. Walk across the beach, setting for Picnic 11 (and also visited in Walks 17 and 19). On the opposite side is a fine beach bar and restaurant, the Cafeteria Susy (open from late April to October). The café also provides toilets and shower. To continue the walk, begin the steep ascent of a splendid wooden staircase with no less than 214 steps. Bear left at the top along a wide path.

Some 13 minutes along the track forks. Turn left, clambering down over rocks, skirting a wall on your left (as you have done since the path reached the top of the cliff). Two minutes later do something similar (there are waymarks, and you may spot a red dot on a stone as well). During the next eight minutes ignore occasional paths to the right, and continue to follow the wide track beside the wall (photograph page 99). Eventually you will come to a crossing wall. There are two gaps in it. Go down to the lower one **(4h07min)** *(15min)*. (Or, easier but less scenic and slightly longer, follow the directions from the 4h44min-point in Walk 17.) Ignore the track to the left, and follow the stony path down the side of the cliff towards **Cala Santa Galdana** (photograph page 98). Soon you will pass the end of a footbridge and go down steps to the road beside the HOTEL AUDAX. Follow the road beside the river towards a large car park just beyond the roundabout. The BUS STOP is next to the CAR PARK **(4h22min)**.

Cala Santa Galdana to Cala'n Bosch

Distance: 16km/10mi; 4h32min
How to get there: 🚌 to Cala Santa Galdana. It may be necessary to go to Ferreries first. Or 🚗 (only possible if you intend to walk part way and then re-trace your steps to Cala Santa Galdana). Drive to Cala Santa Galdana. At the roundabout as you enter the resort, take the middle road down into the town and turn right over the bridge. Park in the large car park on the right.
To return: 🚌 from Cala'n Bosch or 🚗 from Cala Santa Galdana

Leaving the BUS STOP OR CAR PARK in **Cala Santa Galdana**, turn left, and **begin** by walking towards the sea, keeping to the right of the river (map pages 96-97). Ahead of you, beyond the HOTEL AUDAX, steps take you to the base of the cliff and to a footpath which climbs past the end of a footbridge and up the side of the cliff in the setting shown on page 98. In five minutes go through a gap in a wall (**15min**) *(4h07min),* and very shortly turn left along a wide track. For the next 12 minutes you will skirt to the left of the drystone wall.

The good Camí de Cavalls waymarking will prove helpful to you at critical moments for the whole of this walk. Climb over some rocks and turn right along a wide crossing track, still beside the wall (photograph page 99). In a couple of minutes do something similar, and two minutes after that begin to walk away from the wall. After 10 minutes the track turns right; descend the 214 steps of an imposing wooden staircase to **Cala Macarella**, the setting for Picnic 11 and also visited on Walks 17 and 19. You pass the end of the garden of a fine beach bar and restaurant, Cafeteria Susy, open from late April to October (**40min**) *(3h34min).*

Cross the beach and go over the water drain. You will meet a number of similar water courses, which prevent the ends of the *barrancs* forming marshes. To your left you will notice, halfway up the cliff face and overlooking the sea, a couple of CAVES and the wide ledge that leads to them — doubtless highly desirable residences in Menorca's troglodytic period. To your right, at the foot of the cliff, is an iron gate barring access to a track leading to the Macarella estate (closed to walkers). A green arrow here points to a second path, immediately to the left of the gate, which otherwise would be hidden. Its great age is evident by the depth to which it is eroded.

Walk up this path away from Macarella Beach, and in two minutes pass through a gap in a wall. Carry on ahead, ignoring a path on the left in two minutes. In another two minutes you will reach a T-junction. Here turn left and, 50m/yds further on, fork left. Follow this path to the END OF THE HEADLAND (about 200m/yds), for the views you get over two *calas*. Then retrace your steps for 100m/yds and turn left along the narrow waymarked path. The path goes straight to the edge of the cliff, where a stone staircase has been cut from the rock by which you descend to **Cala Macarelleta**'s little gem of a beach, shown on page 104 (**56min**) *(3h16min).*

If you can bear to leave Cala Macarelleta, walk to the left of the back of the beach, and up a wide path along the side of a small valley. Ignore a path on the right. After ten minutes further walking there is a section of eroded track that has been repaired with concrete, and just beyond it ignore a turning to the left. A minute later, turn left along the well-trodden path (**1h13min**) *(3h06min).* Two buildings can be seen ahead: the medieval WATCHTOWER OF **Artruix**, and the cream-coloured Mallauí farmhouse. Nine minutes later the path goes through a gate in a wall, and in five minutes forks. Turn right along the wider path, descend through woodland, and finally emerge on the beach of **Cala'n Turqueta** (**1h36min**) *(2h 44min)*. *(The Shorter walk returns here.)*

To continue the walk, pass the toilets and go through the car park. Turn sharply left at the end and walk back beside the car park wall. Half way along, turn right. In a couple of minutes ignore a turning to the right that goes through a wall, and shortly go through a gateway. Turn left and descend. When you are nearly at the edge of the cliff, turn right through what appear to be the remains of a former building. Climb over a broken section of wall, then go up steps on the other side. Turn right. In 2-3 minutes, no more, turn left along a little path. It is waymarked, but very easy to miss. A minute later, ignore a narrow path going uphill to the right. In five minutes the path will have brought you to a wall. Turn left. After 50m/yds the path veers away from the wall, and in another 50m/yds you ignore a path to the right. For 13 minutes the path will take you along the coastline before finally turning back to the wall. Turn left now, but in seven minutes turn left down a narrow path that brings you to the back of another lovely little beach, that of **Cala d'es Talaier** (**2h21min**) *(2h)*.

At the far end of the beach, ignore a wide path on your right (it cuts across the next headland); follow the *Camí* round the cliffs until you emerge at **Platja de Son Saura** (**2h37min**) *(1h40min)*. This large beach is one of the most beautiful on the coast. It is the setting for Picnic 20 and the starting- and finishing-point for the Shorter walk.

When you are ready to leave Son Saura beach, walk round the edge towards the rock outcrop on the far side,

WATCHTOWERS
All the coastal walks in the book will take you past at least one watchtower. Some of them date back as early as the 16th century and were built to try to avert future disasters on the scale of the Turkish assaults of 1535 (see page 33) and 1558 (see page 113). Others were built by the British or French during the wars of the 18th century, while yet more were built by the British during the Napoleonic War at the beginning of the 19th century.
The tiny, cylindrical towers you will come across from time to time are the remains of windmills. Some have been partially restored and turned to other uses, like those seen on page 25 at Sant Lluís (Walk 12) and page 113 at Ciutadella (Walk 20).

Photograph: the Atalaia d'Artruix (Walks 18 and 19)

and cross another marsh-draining water course. Turn left and follow the path over the rock outcrop to the second half of the beach. Walk round that until you come to a wall, go through the gate and keep straight ahead (ignoring first a track to the left, then one to the right). You are now on an ancient cart track which runs to an old slipway. Cross the slipway, and follow a path for 200m/yds to the next bay. Walk round this bay, which is guarded at both ends by BLOCKHOUSES, then make your way across the rocky headland and on between a shrubby area on your right and the sea on your left. As you continue westwards across this rocky terrain you will pass between a pair of CAVES. The one on the left is rather nice, with a pilaster and central pillar. Two minutes beyond the caves, go through a gateway (**3h22min**) *(1h01min)*.

Go ahead now, on a good track. Follow it inland for six minutes, then turn left down another ancient track leading to the sea. In 100m/yds look out for a SMALL MEGALITHIC ENCLOSURE on your right, and follow the track round past a squatters' summer camp. Do not go all the way down to the sea, but turn right and follow the path round the back of bushes and across more rocky ground towards a wall. Ignore the path on the right, and go through a gap in the wall, to continue with a wall to your right and **Punta Prima** to your left. In six minutes go through a wooden gate (**3h42min**) *(45min)*.

Pass a small white building. Steps beside it lead to a mooring in a cave below. The building houses the machinery for raising a boat out of the water. Walk next round **Cala Parejals**, where the cliffs are steadily crumbling into the sea. Pass through a gateway and walk parallel with the sea for 100m/yds. Ignore a track to the right, and for another 0.5km/0.3mi walk between bushes with the sea on your left, to arrive at the beach of **Son Xoriguer** (**4h07min**) *(20min)*. Round the beach and leave the CAR PARK at the far end by following paths on the far side. This will bring you to the final beach, at **Cala'n Bosch**. On the far side stands the Cala'n Bosch Hotel. Walk past it to the BUS STOP in front of the hotel entrance (**4h32min**).

Walk 19: ES PUJOL DE SON TICA AND CALA MACARELLA

See also map on pages 96-97 and cover photograph

Distance: 17.5km/10.8mi; 4h35min

Grade: moderate, on account of the length; mostly on country roads (watch for motorists making for the beach!), with a short stretch along the coast

Equipment: comfortable footwear, sunhat, raingear, suncream, picnic, plenty of water, swimwear, towel

How to get there and return: 🚗 only accessible by car or taxi. Driving to Ciutadella from the Mahón direction, turn left at the roundabout as you reach the town, following signs for the beaches of Macarella and Turqueta. Park on the left after 5km at Sant Joan de Missa, shown on page 111.

Shorter walk: Sant Joan de Missa — Cala Macarella — Cala Santa Galdana (11km/6.8mi; 3h10min). Grade, equipment as main walk. Access: 🚕 taxi from Ciutadella to the Ermita de Sant Joan de Missa. Follow the main walk to the 2h15min-point. Then turn to page 105 and follow Walk 18 from the 3h34min-point to the end (map pages 96-97; photograph page 98). Return by 🚌 from Cala Santa Galdana to Ciutadella (via Ferreries).

This walk starts at the picturesque country church (*ermita*) of Sant Joan de Missa (St John the Baptist). This *ermita* seems to have been built shortly after the Reconquest of Menorca from the Moors by Alfonso III in 1287 and occupies an important place in local folklore. The walk circles a region known as Es Pujol de Son Tica and visits three lovely beaches.

To begin, leave **Sant Joan de Missa** and turn right (west), walking back to the T-junction. At the junction, turn left along the CAMI DE SON CAMARO. In **10min** you pass the entrance to the farm of SON FOCU on the left and immediately come to a T-junction. Take the road to the *right* (our original route, the quieter lane to the left, is now closed to walkers beyond the farm of Al Para). In just over 4km keep right at a fork (where MARJAL NOVA and SANT FRANCESC are to the left). Under 500m further on you come to a first, large parking area for the beach. *Referring now to the map on pages 96-97,* follow the track down through woodland to the pretty beach of **Cala'n Turqueta** (**1h25min**).

From the beach, walk past the toilets at the seaward end of the lower car park and bear left to climb up a sandy path. For a few minutes you rise through a pine wood, before emerging into more open country. Now the path bends left; ignore a path on the right. The path winds through low bushes to a wall, where you pass through a gateway. Keep straight ahead now, with a wall on your left. After another seven minutes the path has widened and brought you to a major junction, where you turn right (**1h48min**). Shortly, ignore a path off left and two paths on the right, and descend through a small valley that bring you to another superb little beach, **Cala Macarelleta** (**1h58min**).

Cross to the left-hand side of the beach (as you face the sea), then take the steps cut into the rock, which turn left and wind

their way up to the top of the cliff. From the top of the steps a short path leads to a T-junction with a broad path. Your way is left, but before leaving, walk in the opposite direction to the END OF THE HEADLAND, where you have splendid views over both Macarelleta beach and its larger neighbour, Macarella.

Retrace your steps and pass the short path. Two minutes later, when the path turns right, ignore a path on the left, and in 50m/yds turn right down a rocky path. Go through a gap in a wall and descend to emerge at the rear of **Cala Macarella** (**2h15min**; Picnic 11), also visited on Walks 17 and 18. From late April to October you will find sustenance at Cafeteria Susy.

Walk to the rear of the beach and go through the CAR PARK. Continue along the track as it makes its way up the beautiful **Barranc de Santa Anna**, spoiled only by the many cars that now use it. After 20 minutes pass on your right the entrance to SANTA ANNA farm, and 25 minutes later make your way past TORRALBA farm on your left. From now on the road is metalled. After a further 20 minutes you will reach TORRALBET farm (the 3h28min-point in Walk 17). *Referring again to the map above,* bear left along the tarmac road (**3h20min**). In 10 minutes you

CHAPELS

Outside the island's small towns there are few villages. There are however several small churches dotted about the countryside at central locations to which farming families can come for mass. They are known as *ermitas* ('hermitages'). Walk 19 begins at the *ermita* shown above. Walk 1 passes another *ermita* dedicated to St John the Baptist, Walk 9 that of Sant Llorenç (St Laurence), and Walk 14 that of Santa Maria (Saint Mary).

In the past even these churches were too difficult for some families to get to. Sometimes it was easier to bring the priest to the family, and occasionally you will notice a chapel built next to a remote farmhouse, as at Binissaida on Walk 6. Finally, Walks 7, 8 and 11 take you to what remains of two churches built in the very early days of Christianity, at Es Fornàs (page 60) and Son Bou (page 76).

pass the gate to PABOR-DIA VELLA on the right. Beyond here the pine woods on your left decline, and the road dips to the right, to cross a low valley. After climbing out, the road bends left and eventually you pass the entrance to MOR-VEDRA VEI (**4h**), an old fortified farm (see panel page 129). Again the road turns left, soon passing MORVEDRA NOU, a rural hotel/restaurant. It is all downhill now, and in 25 minutes you reach **Sant Joan de Missa** (**4h35min**).

Photograph: Sant Joan de Missa. Every year the people of Ciutadella celebrate the birthday of St John the Baptist on 24 June with splendid displays of horsemanship in which more than 100 riders take part. The ceremonies begin on the eve of the festival, with all the horsemen riding out to this church to sing the evening service.

Walk 20: A WALKABOUT TOUR OF CIUTADELLA

See town plan pages 114-115; see also illustrations pages 27, 122-4, 126

Distance: 5km/3mi for those travelling by bus; under 7km/4.3mi if you arrive by car; about 3h

Grade: easy

Equipment: comfortable shoes of any sort, sunhat, raingear, suncream

How to get there and return: 🚌 or 🚐 to/from Ciutadella. 🚌: Approaching Ciutadella along the Me-1, turn left at the horse roundabout shown on page 27. There is a car park to your left. Walk back to the horse roundabout, turn left and follow the Camí de Maó to the Plaça de Ses Palmeres. I find this by far the most convenient place to park, but it adds just under 1km each way to the walk. There is also car parking in the Plaça d'es Born (if you arrive early enough), in which case start the tour at [4]. Visitors coming in from the beaches on the Torres 🚐 should start at the Plaça de S'Esplanada [9]; see page 117.Those arriving on the TMSA 🚐 from the Mahón direction should begin at the Plaça dels Pins [10]; see page 117

The dismantling of the city walls was begun in 1868, so that 'the Citadel of Menorca' could expand. Their line is marked by a series of wide avenues which divide the old city from the modern part. Our walk lies mostly within the confines of the old city, which is where the most impressive and important buildings are to be found. Care must be taken to follow the route exactly as described, for it meanders through the maze of narrow streets which give Ciutadella its very special character, wherein aristocrat and artisan live side by side.

The walk begins in the **Plaça de Ses Palmeres** [1]. This square is also called Alfons III, after King Alfonso III of Aragon, nicknamed 'the Liberal', the hero of the Reconquest. Before 1868 the gate to the old city stood on this spot. To left and right, where there are wide avenues today, the massive city walls rose up. Here Alfonso entered Ciutadella in triumph, and every 22 January that event is celebrated. A statue of St Anthony Abad (on whose feast five days earlier the Moors had been vanquished) is carried in a cortège led by three horsemen. One of them bangs on the ground three times with his staff at the entrance to the city, to announce the King's arrival.

On the opposite side of the square from the Camí de Maó is the CARRER DE MAO. This is the beginning of the main street through the town. Before starting along it, turn round and look back at the corner of the Camí de Maó, where the WINDMILL shown opposite has been turned into a popular bar. One of the chief attractions of Ciutadella is apparent as you walk between the houses which frame the entrance to Carrer de Maó — its many elegant buildings.

Some pleasant shops are to be found in Carrer de Maó, before it opens out into the delightful **Plaça Nova**. Walk along the left-

ABOUT THE CITY

As far as the British were concerned, Menorca was an appendage to Port Mahón. Most other rulers of the island preferred the harbour of Ciutadella. Although by no means so deep nor so long as that of Mahón, the port of Ciutadella was adequate for the shallow draught shipping of former times, and it had the advantage of being nearer both to Mallorca and mainland Spain. So it was here that the largest fortified city of the island grew up, hence its name 'Citadel'.

The history of the city begins in the time of the Carthaginians, who knew it as Iamno. In 123 BC, Quintus Caecilius Metellus was sent by the Senate of Rome to suppress the Balearic pirates, which was sufficient excuse for him to add the islands to the Roman Empire (and reward himself by taking the title 'Balearicus'). Ciutadella changed its name slightly to Iamona, and 140km (85mi) of roads were built across Menorca to link it with other Roman forts at Santa Agueda and Mahón. The first Islamic raid occurred as early as 707, when Moorish pirates came in search of slaves, but the conquest of Menorca was delayed for two more centuries, until it was added to the Emirate of Cordova in 902. The Kaid, as the Muslim governor was called, chose Ciutadella to be his capital. He built his palace, the Alcazar, overlooking the harbour. For nearly four centuries the Moors knew the city by the Arabic name of Medina Minurka — 'The City of Menorca', and here they built their chief mosque. At the Reconquest in 1287 Alfonso III of Aragon entered Ciutadella on 22 January and declared it the island's capital. Throughout the remainder of the Middle Ages there was continual rivalry between Ciutadella and Mahón, as the latter grew steadily in importance.

The most momentous event in Ciutadella's history took place in the year 1558, when 150 Turkish ships under the command of Barbarossa's

Northeast corner of Born Square (top), the harbour (above) and the windmill/bar on the Camí de Maó

successor Piali, carrying 15,000 troops, sailed into the port. After nine days' siege the city fell. Its 3495 inhabitants, including the governor Don Bartolome Arguimbau, were taken as slaves to Constantinople, and the city was sacked so completely that when a new governor came out, he was compelled to spend his first night in a cave — there were no houses left standing in Ciutadella.

But the city was rebuilt, and many of the captives were ransomed and returned home. However, even before the coming of the British in 1708, the governor moved his residence to Mahón, which served to intensify the rivalry between the two cities.

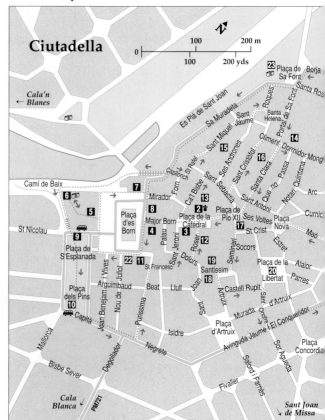

hand side of the square, and continue into the narrow SES VOLTES (also called J M Quadrado), bordered on each side with arcades. These arches *(voltes)* are a feature of Ciutadella. At the end of Ses Voltes you come to **Plaça de Pio XII**.

Carry on in the same direction into **Plaça de la Catedral**, passing **St Mary's Cathedral** [2] on your right. This was where the Moors built their principal mosque. As soon as Alfonso expelled them, the mosque was consecrated as a Christian church, as were all other mosques on the island. Gradually a new Christian church was built to replace it, being completed in 1362. All that remains today of the Moorish building is part of the minaret, which was incorporated into the tower on the north side. The church is enclosed within a windowless curtain wall, which may be part of the original building or may have been added after the Turkish destruction to provide extra defence. So damaged was the building at that time that restoration took 150 years. The contrasting west entrance is a neo-classical addition

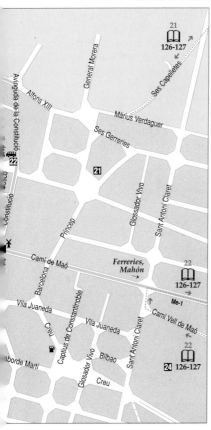

CIUTADELLA — KEY

1 Plaça de Ses Palmeres
2 St Mary's Cathedral (Santa María)
3 Tourist Information Office (Plaça de la Catedral)
4 Salort Palace
5 Ajuntament (Town Hall)
6 Bastió des Governador
7 Teatro Borne
8 Torre-Saura Palace
9 Torres Buses (from the beaches)
10 TMSA Buses (from Mahón)
11 Sant Francesc (St Francis) Church
12 Nuestra Señora del Rosario Church
13 Bishop's Palace
14 Santa Clara Convent
15 San Miguel Church
16 Lluriach Palace
17 Santo Cristo Church
18 Saura Palace
19 Martorell Palace
20 Market
21 Hospital
22 Post Office
23 Bastió de Sa Font
24 Municipal Cemetery

dating from 1813. The interior suffered badly from vandalism at the hands of the Republicans during the Civil War. The TOURIST INFORMATION OFFICE [3] is on your left.

From the square keep going in the same westerly direction along CARRER MAJOR DEL BORN, which leads into one of the finest city squares in the whole of Spain: the **Plaça d'es Born**. Dominating the square, a great obelisk (photograph page 123) commemorates the brave resistance put up by the townspeople to the Turkish attack. The Latin inscription (by Josep María Quadrado) translates 'Here we fought untiI death for our religion and our country in the year 1558'. Turn left on leaving Major del Born and pass on the corner one of the most impressive mansions in Ciutadella

Turn left on leaving Major del Born and pass on the corner one of the most impressive mansions in Ciutadella, the **Salort Palace** [5]. In summer, it is often open to visitors between 10am and 2pm (the entrance is back the way you came, about 30m/yds to the right along Major del Born, through an open, unmarked, wooden door, directly opposite the larger, more imposing entrance to the Torre Saura Palace). Remember to look up: here in Menorca the principal reception rooms are always on the first floor. The great wooden doors at ground level usually open on to spacious courtyards.

Continue your walk round the square until you reach the building opposite, the **Ajuntament** or town hall [5]. To the left of it a passage leads to steps up to a 17th-century tower known as the **Bastió d'es Governador** [6], from where you have a splendid view over the harbour. Note that it is only open in the morning. The town hall was once the governor's palace. The present building is the result of a 19th-century restoration. Its crenellation and round arches, and the palm trees in front, give this corner of Ciutadella a deliberately Moorish appearance: it was here that the Alcazar, the palace of the Kaid, stood for 385 years. Do go inside. Much can be seen, even during working hours. There is a Gothic reception hall with panelled ceiling and wrought-iron lamps, a small museum which contains the battle banner of King Alfonso, and portraits of the city's notable citizens of yesteryear (as well as one of King George III, which the British left behind, and another of the American admiral, David Farragut). After working hours, from 6-8pm (12-1pm on Saturdays) more of the rooms can be viewed. In the mayor's office is the 'Llibre Vermell', the medieval 'Red Book', recording the privileges King Alfonso gave to the island.

St Mary's Cathedral, seen from across the harbour

Facing you across Born Square now, to the left of Carrer Major del Born is the most splendid of all the houses in Ciutadella — the palace of the Count of Torre-Saura. The family coat-of-arms is emblazoned above the doorway (photograph page 123). As you walk along the north side of the square you will see below you what little remains of the medieval fortifications and the lovely harbour. Just before the corner you pass the theatre, the **Teatro Borne** [7]. Turn left after you have finished inspecting the **Torre-Saura Palace** [8] and leave the square by CARRER DE SA MURADETA, which first turns right and then left to bring you to the top of a wide flight of steps that take you down to the harbour. At the bottom turn left and walk along the quayside beneath the great walls, and maybe stop at one of the cafés for refreshment. Then continue alongside the harbour and turn left to follow CARRER MARINA up behind the town hall. Where the street turns left, you will see a flight of steps ahead. Go up these steps.* Cross Camí de Sant Nicolau to the park opposite, the **Plaça de S'Esplanada**. This is where the TORRES BUS STOPS [9] are situated.

Walk away from the bus stops the length of the tree-filled park, leaving the Born Square and its obelisk behind you. This is where the first section of the walls once stood. At the end of the park you come the **Plaça dels Pins** and the STOPS FOR TMSA BUSES from Mahón [10]. You are now at the beginning of the avenues that continue the line of the former walls. The first one is AVINGUDA DEL CAPITA NEGRETE, and here you turn left. Captain Negrete had the misfortune to be the senior army officer in Ciutadella on the day the Turks sailed into the harbour (see 'About the city', page 113). He had under him 40 soldiers whom he had brought from Castille to repair the city's defences. Local territorials brought the number of armed men up to about 620.

Pass two streets, Carrer Joan Benejam i Vives, and Carrer Nou de Juliol, and turn left along the third, CARRER PURISSIMA. This leads back to Born Square where, on the corner with the Plaça d'es Born, is the **Church of Sant Francesc** [11]. Architecturally the church is a mixture of 14th-century Gothic that survived the destruction and restoration baroque. When James II of Mallorca succeeded Alfonso in 1291 (he was only 23 when he died) he appointed a Royal Commission to organise Menorcan affairs which met in this church.

Just before the end of Carrer Purissima, opposite the church,

---

*Recommended diversion (2.1km/1.3mi; 30min): Turn sharply right here and follow the CAMI DE BAIX above the *cala* as far as the 16th-century **Castell de Sant Nicolau** and bust of Admiral Farragut (see page 118). Return to this point either along the Camí de Baix or go down steps by the harbour lights and walk along the landing stage.

turn right along Carrer de Sant Francesc (San Francisco). At the end, turn left along Carrer de Sant Jeroni. This street is bordered on the right by one of the older mansions, that of the Sintas family. At the junction with Carrer dels Dolors turn right and pass (on the left) the Plazuela del Rosario. Turn left along the next street, Carrer Roser: on the right is a visual treat, the gorgeous little church of **Nuestra Señora del Rosario** [12], from which the street gets its name. (This church too was vandalised during the Civil War.) It was begun at the end of the 17th century by the Dominican friars. When the British came in 1708 they requisitioned it and held Church of England services there for the benefit of the British soldiers. The extravagant baroque decoration of the main doorway is, like the Chapel of the Immaculate Conception in Mahón's St Francis Church (see page 38), decidedly churrigueresque . It now hosts exhibitions.

As you make your way to the end of Carrer Roser, you will see the Gothic south door of St Mary's Cathedral facing you. On reaching the **Plaça de la Catedral** once more, cross to the far left-hand corner where, opposite the west entrance to the cathedral, No 8 is the home of the Olives family. This mansion was built early in the 17th century. It contains much fine furniture, some made in the 18th century by Menorcan craftsmen from English pattern books, and some French from the time of the brief French occupation of the island (1756-63). Also French is the frieze featuring birds, animals and fishes which runs round the top of the walls in the three large state rooms.

Turn right and continue along Carrer del Ca'l Bisbe, passing on your right the **Bishop's Palace** [13]. Christianity arrived early in Menorca, and there was a bishopric here until 484, when the last bishop, Makarius, sailed for North Africa to defend his faith before the heretical Vandal king, Hunnericus, never to be heard of again. Not until 1795 did the Vatican restore its bishop to Menorca and, as had been the case in the past, he chose Ciutadella to be the seat of his diocese. Previously his palace had been an Augustinian convent.

Facing the end of the street is yet another fine house, the Squella mansion, home of the Marqués de Menas Albas. It was here that the American Admiral David Farragut slept when he visited Ciutadella in December 1867. The bedroom and bed he used are still preserved. Farragut may well be unknown to English readers, but to Americans he is as important as Nelson. It was during the American Civil War that he made a name for himself, by sinking eleven Confederate warships and capturing New Orleans. He was put in command of all the naval forces and created First Admiral of the US Navy in 1866. The admiral's father was born in Ciutadella and had emigrated to the States when he was seventeen. During a goodwill visit of the American fleet to Mahón harbour, Admiral Farragut took the opportunity to visit his father's birthplace. Ciutadella took him to its heart. He was fêted and made an honorary citizen. There is a bust of him by the harbour mouth, near the Esmeralda Hotel.

Turn right at the junction, into CARRER SANT SEBASTIA. Pass Carrer de ses Andrones on the left, and turn along the next street on the left, CARRER SANT CRISTOFOL. Then take the second street on the right, CARRER CLIMENT, go under the arch and carry on in the same direction along CARRER DEL DORMIDOR DE LES MONGES (Padre Federico Pareja). On the left is the **Santa Clara Convent** [14], founded through the generosity of Alfonso the Liberal in 1287. Destroyed by the Turks, the convent was rebuilt in the 17th century. To finance this, the order imitated a practice initiated by Fr Miguel Subirats, the Prior of the Augustinians, to restore his convent (now the Bishop's Palace). They secured from the King of Spain the privilege of offering deeds of nobility to members of wealthy families in return for contributions. Many of the noble families whose houses you see on the walk acquired their titles in this way. The convent was restored once more in 1945. In 1987, on the 700th anniversary of its foundation, a plaque was put up recording its history.

Turn left along CARRER DE MARIA AUXILIADORA, passing the sanctuary of the Salesian Fathers and, at the end, turn left along AVINGUDA DE FRANCESC DE BORJA MOLL and follow the line of the last section of wall to the **Plaça de Sa Font** or 'Fountain Square'. Here you can see the only section of wall still remaining other than by the harbour.

Walk across the square and go along CARRER DE SA MURADETA to the left of the tower that is home to the municipal museum and was once the reservoir for the city's water supply. The ground falls away steeply on your right, giving a view of small terraced gardens on both slopes of the valley. The wide sandy expanse below is **Es Plá de Sant Joan** (St John the Baptist). Notice how the steps lead down through all the gardens to terraces or platforms beside the wall which look out over Es Plá. That is where Menorca's most prestigious festival takes place annually on June 24th, the feast of St John the Baptist. The ceremony goes back to the Middle Ages. It begins with a cavalcade of over a hundred richly caparisoned horses, their riders *(caixers)* in traditional costume. The cavalcade is led by a man bearing the flag of the Knights of St John of Malta. There follow displays of horsemanship, with prancing steeds, and young men doing their best to make them unseat their riders, all to the accompaniment of pipes and tambourines and general merriment. Then these terraces will be thronged with onlookers getting the best — and safest — view of the proceedings. It is the spirit of this festival that is expressed in the statue seen on page 27.

Towards the end of Carrer de Sa Muradeta, immediately before the steps going down to the port, turn left into CARRER DE PERE CAPLLONCH. Ignore Carrer des Forn on the right, and turn left again into CARRER SANT RAFEL. Now is the time to let your imagination have free rein. If ever there were streets which allowed you to pass back through time, they are these alleyways. But do remember that though the layout of the streets may be medieval, or even Moorish, the houses themselves cannot predate 1558. All had to be rebuilt after the Turkish destruction.

Pass on the right the junction with Carrer Sant Sebastià, and follow the street as it turns first right, then left, into CARRER SANT MIQUEL. On the right you will pass **San Miguel Church** [15]. At the end of the street turn right into CARRER SANT JAUME and, almost at once, go left at the junction with CARRER SANT BARTOMEU. Turn sharply right at the next junction. After 25m/yds turn left into tiny CARRERO DE SANTA HELENA.

Turn right at the T-junction along PORTAL DE SA FONT (Carrer Fuente). Very soon you pass the convent of Santa Clara again, on your left. In the 18th century the convent was the scene of a scandal straight from the pages of a 'Mills and Boon'. The saintly sisters ran a school for young ladies. With the ingenuity of young ladies the world over, three of the pupils managed both to make the acquaintance of, and to fall in love with, a trio of young English army officers. With determined recklessness, the girls fled the convent and hid with the lieutenants, rejecting all attempts to persuade them to return. The Roman Catholic church was up in arms. The girls must be returned to the convent. The governor, General Blakeney, showing a remarkable broadness of mind, refused to force them back against their will. All were duly wed and, I suppose, lived happily ever after.

Keep going in the same direction and enter CARRER SANTA CLARA. On your right, No 29 is one of the oldest and most prestigious of the stately homes — **Lluriach Palace** [16], home of the Barons of Lluriach, the oldest of the Menorcan titles. Its facade shows that stern rejection of ostentation characterising so many Spanish buildings. It is impressive nonetheless.

At the end of Carrer Santa Clara cross over Ses Voltes (Carrer J M Quadrado) and go along CARRER D'ES SEMINARI. There are three fine buildings here, all on your left. The first is **Santo Cristo Church** [17], a tiny baroque gem, built in 1667 and restored in 1967. Outside are classical columns and capitals and an octagonal stone dome surmounted by a stone lantern. Within there is a tiny gallery. Lower down the street is a bank which is housed in one of the town's former mansions — a mansion with a story. The

British first came to Menorca because of their involvement in the War of the Spanish Succession. King Carlos II of Spain had died childless, and there were two young claimants to the throne, descended from his sisters. One was French, Prince Philip of Anjou, the other Austrian, the Archduke Charles. Inevitably Britain was determined that it could not be the Frenchman. In the war that ensued, the Royal Navy was hampered by having to return to England every winter, and General James Stanhope saw the value to Britain in having the use of Mahón harbour. He gained the support of the pro-Austrian party on Menorca, whose leader was Juán Miguel Saura y Morell. In revenge the pro-French party burned his home to the ground. After Stanhope had conquered the island, he had a splendid new house built in Ciutadella for Saura — the one occupied today by the bank. The third building is another church towards the end of the street, now the diocesan museum.

Turn right at the end of Carrer d'es Seminari into CARRER SANTISSIM. Halfway along pass a street on the left (Artruix), which you will eventually follow. But before doing so, walk to the end of the street and look at the building on your left. Now partly an antique shop, it is **Saura Palace** [18], built towards the end of the 17th century. It is finely proportioned, with beautiful neo-classical decorations round the full-length windows on the first floor. Inside is a broad staircase made in 1718, and the reception rooms are lit by magnificent chandeliers made in La Granja, near Madrid. On the other side of Carrer Santissim is **Martorell Palace** [19], home of the Marqués de Albranca. Like Lluriach Palace, its façade is reserved in decoration, exhibiting again that Spanish architectural puritanism.

Return now to the street you passed earlier, and turn along CARRER DEL PORTAL D'ARTRUIX. Shortly, take the first turning on the left, CARRER CASTELL RUPIT. After some 80m/yds you reach the **Plaça de la Libertat**, built in 1868 and today home to the MARKET [20], sadly in decline since the arrival of supermarkets. At the end of Carrer Castell Rupit turn right along CARRER SANT ONOFRE and, after crossing one street, you will come to the AVINGUDA JAUME I EL CONQUERIDOR. 'Conqueror' is the title bestowed on King James I of Aragon for the reconquest of Catalonia and Mallorca. He began the reconquest of Menorca which his grandson Alfonso completed. He did not actually invade the smaller island, but terrified its Moorish rulers into becoming his vassals.

Turn left along Conqueridor and bear left into AVINGUDA DE LA CONSTITUCIO for some 200m/yds, back to the **Plaça de Ses Palmeres** (2-3h). Those who started at [4], [9] or [10] should now turn back to [1] on page 112 and continue from there.

Walk 21: A COUNTRY STROLL FROM CIUTADELLA

See town plan on pages 114-115, then map on pages 126-127
Distance: up to 6km/3.7mi; under 2h *from the Plaça d'es Born* (allow another 2km if you park near the 'horse roundabout').

Grade: easy

Equipment: comfortable shoes of any sort, sunhat, raingear, suncream

How to get there and return: as Walk 20, page 112; begin at the Born Square (Plaça d'es Born).

T his short walk — especially suitable for an evening *paseo* before the late dinner — is a pleasant alternative to strolling round the old city and gives you a taste of rural Menorca.

Start the walk by crossing the **Plaça d'es Born**. Pass the obelisk, and leave by CARRER DE SA MURADETA in the corner nearest the harbour. Walk along that street past the steps leading down to the port and continue to the end, looking down on the sandy Plá de Sant Joan. When you reach the old tower/museum (**Bastió de Sa Font**), continue along AVINGUDA DE FRANCESC DE BORJA MOLL opposite. Cross over AVINGUDA DE LA CONSTITUCIO and continue along CARRER ALFONS XIII. Keep left at the end and continue in the same direction along CARRER DE MARIO VERDAGUER, named for Menorca's foremost man of letters.

Turn left after 100m/yds on the CAMI DE SES CAPELLETES, and you are suddenly in farming country (**12min**). Keep right at the fork after 70m/yds, to walk below Carrer Sant Antoni Claret. Some 80m/yds from the underpass, when the road bends sharp left towards a roundabout, keep ahead on a bit of track to the ring road (RC-1). Referring now to the map on pages 126-127, climb the barrier and cross with care. Another bit of track beyond the barrier will bring you back to the lane.

Fountain in the Plaça d'es Born

Cattle shed north of the Me-1, opposite the naveta at Es Tudons (Walk 22)

CATTLE SHEDS

When a walk takes you through farming country, you will frequently come across small drystone buildings that look like miniature Babylonian ziggurats. These are cattle sheds and are known as *ponts*.

Since Menorca totally lacks building timber, all roofing until recent times was done with stones, hence the need to narrow the span to be covered in this imaginative and unusual way.

It is claimed that some have recently been built to provide homes, not for cattle, but for people, since they do not require planning permission!

Entrance to the Torre-Saura Palace (top) and obelisk in the Plaça d'es Born

After 150m/yds you come to a junction: take either of the lanes forking ahead (rather than those off at right angles), and follow it into increasingly remote and pleasant countryside. As farm after farm peels off, so the tracks become narrower until, reaching the last farm, they end. Each route takes about 30 minutes. If you only do one, you can probably retrace your steps to the **Plaça d'es Born** in little over **1h**; if you explore both, allow under **2h**.

Walk 22: THE NAVETA D'ES TUDONS AND THE POBLAT OF TORRE TRENCADA

See also town plan pages 114-115 and photographs on pages 122, 123

Distance: 20km/12.4mi; 4h40min

Grade: easy

Equipment: comfortable footwear, sunhat, suncream, raingear, picnic, torch, binoculars, plenty of water

How to get there and return: 🚌 to/from Ciutadella. 🚗 Approaching Ciutadella along the Me-1, turn left at the horse roundabout shown on page 27. There is a car park on your left. Turn right along the Camí Vell on leaving the car park, and join the walk at the 20min-point.

Shorter and alternative walks

1 **Naveta d'es Tudons** (11km/6.8mi; 2h37min; easy; access and equipment as main walk). Follow the main walk to the 1h20min-point, then turn to the 3h23min-point and carry on from there.

2 **Naveta d'es Tudons — Torre Trencada — Naveta d'es Tudons** (9.5km/ 5.9mi; 2h20min; easy). Access only by 🚗: park in the *naveta* car park and walk to the *naveta*. Begin the walk at the 1h20min-point and finish at the 3h23min-point. Return via the *naveta* to the car park.

3 **Naveta d'es Tudons — Torre Trencada — Ciutadella**. 15km/9.3mi; 3h30min; easy). Access by bus or taxi only. 🚐 to the Naveta d'es Tudons. Visit the *naveta* and follow the walk from the 1h20min-point to the end.

4 **Naveta d'es Tudons — Ciutadella** (5.7km/3.5mi; 1h30min; easy). Access by bus or taxi only. 🚐 to the Naveta d'es Tudons. Visit the *naveta*, then carry on across the field to the gate and cattle grid. Turn right and pick up the main walk at the 3h23min-point; follow it to the end.

5 **Naveta d'es Tudons — Cala Galdana**. 15.5km/9.6mi; 4h15min; moderate). Access by bus or taxi only. 🚐 to the Naveta d'es Tudons. Follow the main walk from the 1h20min-point to the 2h20min-point. Then follow Walk 17 from the 2h29min-point (page 97) to the end. Return by 🚐 as Walk 17.

The most celebrated cyclopean building on Menorca is the large burial chamber visible on the left, four kilometres short of Ciutadella as you approach from Ferreries. Various claims have been made for it, including that it is the oldest roofed

Ciutadella: Ses Voltes

THE NAVETA D'ES TUDONS

In the 1950s the *naveta* was in a lamentable condition and in danger of total destruction. It was overgrown with bushes, and one end was broken open. Its present splendid state is due to the enthusiasm of two people.

One was Luís Pericot García, Professor of Archaeology at the University of Barcelona, who conceived and masterminded the restoration. The other was María Luisa Serra Belabre, then Director of Mahón Museum, to whom the work was entrusted. She was aided by an architect named Victor Tolor.

A grant from the March Foundation in 1958 made the work possible, and the excavation of the site and restoration of the *naveta* was undertaken in 1959/60. Bushes were removed, fallen stones restored to their proper places, and additional stones obtained from the same quarry whence the original ones had come. During the excavations María Serra found hundreds of human bones, from at least a hundred bodies, lying on a bed of pebbles. Bronze bracelets still encircled some of the arm bones. Other bronze items and simple jewellery that had been buried with the corpses were also found.

The entrance is narrow and low, but not difficult, and inside there is a vestibule and two chambers, one above the other, both of which were used for burials.

Photograph: the Naveta d'es Tudons

building in Spain, or indeed Europe. It is certainly a very interesting edifice, and the best of the *navetas,* in that it contains two storeys and has been extensively restored. This walk not only visits the *naveta,* but takes you on to another important cyclopean site, the *poblat* of Torre Trencada.

Referring to the plan on pages 114-115, **begin the walk** in BORN SQUARE in **Ciutadella**. Enter MAJOR DEL BORN and walk straight across the old town to the PLAÇA DE SES PALMERES.

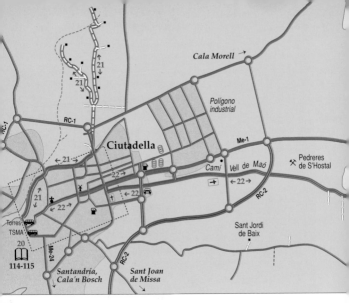

Cross the bypass and keep ahead to the right of the windmill along CAMI DE MAO. Keep straight ahead at the horse roundabout, but turn right at the next one. Walk between the sports hall and the swimming baths and turn left along the CAMI VELL DE MAO (**20min**). Those who came by car will begin here. After passing the new CEMETERY, look out for three *talayots* in a field on your left, and use one of the zebras to cross a major road. After passing below the RC-2 ring road, continue along the lane through a region of QUARRIES. Some are still being worked, others put to a variety of other uses. The most interesting of these are the S'Hostal Quarries (**Pedreres de S'Hostal**), which have been adopted by a group of enthusiasts known as 'Líthica'. The older quarries have been transformed into a botanical garden, while the 20th-century ones are preserved as an example of a working quarry, and occasionally used as an open-air theatre.

Further along the road you will pass the place where the contents of the bins into which you have carefully separated your refuse are taken to be recycled. Another 25 minutes walking will bring you within sight of the massive old farmhouse of ES TUDONS. Opposite the entrance, go over a cattle grid on your left and through a gate. Follow the path and in 200m/yds you will see the **Naveta d'es Tudons** on your left (**1h20min**).

When you leave the *naveta*, retrace your steps and follow the

The Palacio Son Saura in Ciutadella

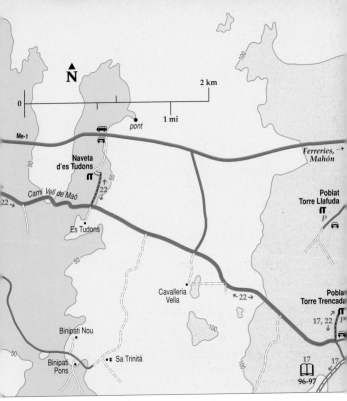

path for 200m/yds, until you reach the field gate and cattle grid and emerge on the tarmac road opposite the entrance to Es Tudons farm. Turn left and follow the lane for 20 minutes, to a road junction. The road to the left brings the traffic from the Me-1, and the lane will be a little busier now, but not too busy.

Under half an hour's walking from here should see you at the car park for the *poblat*, or prehistoric village, of **Torre Trencada**. It is another eight minutes' walking along a signposted path before you come to the site, also visited on Walk 17 (**2h20min**; Picnic 13).

Make your way back to the car park and turn right. Retrace your steps now along the country lane, passing the farm of CAVALLERIA VELLA after 25 minutes. Five minutes later you will lose the traffic returning to the Me-1, and the walk will be much quieter. In 25 minutes you will be back at **Es Tudons** and passing the field gate at the end of the path to the *naveta* (**3h23min**). As you climb the hill on the far side of the valley,

Red kite

Threshing floor near Fornells

THRESHING FLOORS

Just about every farm you pass on your walks will have near it a low, circular, raised stone platform. These are old threshing floors. Weighted sledges would be dragged round by oxen or donkeys over the cut corn, separating the wheat grains from the chaff as they did so. Throwing the mixture into the wind with broad shovels completes the process.

Below: Torre d'en Quart (Walk 23)

THRESHING FLOORS; FORTIFIED FARMS

notice the circular stone THRESHING FLOORS near the farms on your right (**3h50min**). As you get closer to the city, Ciutadella comes into sight, the cathedral prominent. Raise your eyes and beyond the city you will see the distant fortified farmhouse of Torre del Ram. One thing to keep your eyes alert for during this long walk are birds. Large birds especially. I have seen more kites, vultures and eagles flying over or perched beside this road than on any other walk on the island. Or anywhere else for that matter.

Eventually the road will bring you back to the city. The road you have walked along is the CAMI VELL DE MAO, the Old Mahon Road. It was first built by the Romans and continued to be used until Sir Richard Kane built the new road in the 18th century. Walk straight ahead when you come to the SPORTS HALL. This will bring motorists back to the CAR PARK where they will end the walk.

Those who travelled by bus should cross the dual carriageway and, at the final T-junction, turn right along CARRER SANT ANTONI M CLARET. At the traffic lights, turn left along the CAMI DE MAO. Carry on to the PLAÇA DE SES PALMERES and retrace your steps across the old city to the **Plaça d'es Born** (**4h40min**) and nearby BUS STOPS.

Walk 23: CURNIOLA, CALA DE ALGAIARENS AND THE CAVES OF CALA MORELL

See also drawing on page 12

Distance: 14km/8.7mi; 3h45min

Grade: moderate

Equipment: walking boots (preferably, otherwise comfortable shoes or trainers), sunhat, raingear, suncream, picnic, plenty of water, swimwear, towel, binoculars

How to get there and return: 🚌 to/from Cala Morell. Drive from Ferreries towards Ciutadella on the Me-1 and turn right at a roundabout just before the 43km marker.

Alternative walk: Camí de Cavalls (12km/7.4mi; 3h20min; grade, access and equipment as main walk). The main walk has been designed as a circuit, but you can do an out-and-back on the Camí de Cavalls from Cala Morell. Pick up the trail at the roundabout at the entrance to the village, following Via Lactia 500m/yds northeast to the crossing Carrer de Cigne, where you turn right. Then go left almost at once on Carrer del Aguila to the 'official' start of the trail. Return the same way, then follow the main walk from the 3h15min-point.

This lovely walk makes a very wide circuit round the impressive farmhouse of Curniola, partly through agricultural land and partly through pine woods, and then goes on to explore one of the most important Bronze Age cave settlements in Europe. As a bonus, there are opportunities to enjoy a swim in the clearest water surrounding Menorca. The main walk is circular, the first 6km on lightly-trafficked tarmac; you return along the coastal 'road', the Camí de Cavalls.

Begin the walk at **Cala Morell**: head back TOWARDS CIUTA-DELLA along the road by which you have come. As you pass the entrance to CURNIOLA (**9min**), you have your first glimpse of the imposing villa which will pass again near the end of the walk. A minute later you are opposite another farmhouse — BINI ATRAM, while ahead and to the right you can see one of the most famous farmhouses on the island, the massively defended TORRE

FORTIFIED FARMHOUSES

Sometimes you will walk past farmhouses that are attached to large, square, virtually windowless towers. These sturdy dwellings are a feature of the island.

Found also on the mainland in Catalonia, they remind us that Menorca's *calas* attracted quite a different kind of foreign visitor in earlier times — pirates!

The most famous fortified farmhouse on the island is the Torre d'en Quart (left), which you will see during the course of Walk 23.

The fortified farmhouse at Binissaida, shown on page 23, is seen on Walks 4, 6 and 12. Walk 19 passes another good example, Morvedrá Vei.

D'EN QUART (see below). If you didn't stop there on your way in, do so on the way back. Its tower is enormous.

Some **30min** after leaving Cala Morell the main road turns right, past the Torre d'en Quart, towards Ciutadella. A walled-in track goes left to Son Seu farm and Bini Atram. The owners of Bini Atram definitely do *not* welcome walkers on their property — which has led to a rerouting (and improvement!) of this circuit. Continue straight past the Ciutadella road on a narrower, little-trafficked road through farmlands, passing the farm of SON ANGEL on the right. Then, leaving the fields behind you, walk through pines and pass the CASA GUARDA DE SON ANGELS on the left, before turning left down to **Cala de Algaiarens (1h25min)**, one of the loveliest beaches on the island.

After a swim and a break, walk back the way you came, to the car park and shaded picnic area (Picnic 19). Here you pick up the CAMI DE CAVALLS (see page 100), heading right, then left, round the car park, with pines to your right. The *Camí* then moves northwest through pines to the fishermen's cove of **Cala Fontanelles**. Rounding the invigorating cliffs of the **Punta de s'Apres** on a pine-edged path brings you to another track and the **Codolar de Biniatramp**. One user of an earlier edition described the unusual rocks here as a geologist's delight.

Follow the *Camí* southwest past a SMALL BUILDING **(2h05min)** with a garden full of children's playthings. If it is a Sunday or bank holiday it will be full of children playing on them too. Turn right here, and walk beside the boundary wall as far as

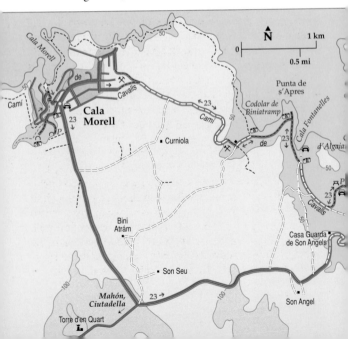

THE CAVES AT CALA MORELL

There are many things to look out for, but their sophistication is probably what impresses most. There are paths chipped out of the rock to provide access to them; often windows light them. Usually a central pillar was left to give support to the roof. Frequently niches and troughs have been carved out, and in several there is a raised area where probably the family slept.

As you move up the valley you will come across even more sophisticated features. There is a channel carved out of the cliff face that directs rainwater down to a trough cut out of the cliff, which overflows into an irrigation channel. Another larger channel collects rainwater on the other side of the valley and conveys it to where it was required for irrigation. One cave has an elaborate façade carved in high relief, to give it the appearance of an Egyptian dwelling. Also of interest are the oval cavities cut into the cliff face. Similar cavities are found all over the island. Local people called them *'capades de Moro'* (drawing page 12) and attributed them to a Moorish passion for head banging! Their purpose can only be guessed at, and it is assumed that it was funerary, perhaps for holding urns containing bones or ashes, or maybe offerings were placed in them. Near the end of the little valley there is a bridge. Go beyond it to the cave on the right. It has two outstanding features — raised sleeping quarters and a magnificently carved chimney. However, by 1000 BC people had moved out of even these fine caves into the 'more fashionable' talayotic settlements, and for the next thousand years they were used for burials.

Cala Morell, from one of the hillside caves

a facing wall. If you look closely, you will see that what was formerly a gap has been walled in, so that now you must climb over to get into the field. Cross the field in the same northwesterly direction, past a worked-out sand QUARRY and on towards woodland. At the far side of the field the track swings left, enters the pine wood and doubles back to the right, skirting the wood. There are plenty of open shady places to rest, or picnic. Some 10 minutes after climbing the wall, the track turns left away from the wood and you reach an iron gate. Beyond the gate the track continues along the edge of a field with shrubs to the right, once more northwestwards, shortly keeping to the right of a wall.

In nine minutes ignore a track on the left (to Curniola); continue to walk beside the wall and, in 20m/yds, go through an iron gate and over a cattle grid. Carry on along the track and go over another cattle grid. Soon you reach the corner of the wall. Ahead is another former sand QUARRY. Walk to the right of the workings *(leaving the Camí de Cavalls)*, heading for the far right-hand corner of the field. Here you climb a low wall into a small field of heather. Follow a path to the nearest concrete post ahead. You will discover that it houses a street lamp. Walk to the end of the street (LLEO MENOR) and turn left into AURIGA. Pass the end of Cassiopea and bear left at the roundabout into VIA LACTIA. After 200m/yds follow VIA LACTIA downhill to the right. Keep straight ahead at the ROUNDABOUT at the entrance to the village (**3h15min**), ignoring the road to Ciutadella on your left, still going downhill. It is not long before you see on your left the first pair of CAVES for which Cala Morell is famous. After exploring these, carry on down the hill, to where a bridge crosses over the *barranc*. The main troglodytic village is situated just before this bridge. Footpaths fork to each side of the hill on your left, and both lead to caves. Most of them are on the left, where they are to be found in the cliffs on both sides of a small valley (Picnic 4).

When you have seen this central part of the village, return to the road and go up the path to the right of the hill. You will soon see two caves some distance away, but as you walk towards them you will discover what seem to be tiny paths cut out from the rock and, when you reach the caves, there is quite an elaborate road carved to the left of them. These caves connect, and the one on the left is surrounded with little stone troughs.

When you have done with the caves, you may wish to sample Cala Morell's other attraction, its swimming. Return to the road, cross the bridge, and immediately fork right. At the next junction turn right and follow the road down to the beach (a gate part way down prohibits cars). As well as the beach, there is a system of rock paths and sunbathing terraces.

From here steps take you back up to restaurants, bars, and the *urbanización*. The last is rather chic. The street lamps are concealed in what look like concrete gnomes watching your progress through the village. If they all work, it could look very romantic after dark. Finally return to your CAR (**3h45min**).

Destinations in the bus timetables on pages 133-134

Numbers following the place names below refer to **timetable** numbers.

BUS TIMETABLES

Most buses are operated by Transportes Menorca SA (TMSA; **www.transportesmenorca. net** or **www.tmsa.es**). The main bus stations are in Mahón and Ciutadella (see page 7). Other operators are Torres (**www.e-torres.net**) and Autos Fornells (**www. autosfornells.com**). *Timetables often change without notice; obtain up-to-date timetables from the web, the bus stations or the tourist office — especially since there are many more bus services than those shown below. These are summer timetables; services may be less frequent from November to April.* **Journey times are approximate and cumulative.**

SERVICES TO AND FROM MAHON/MAO

1 Mahón—Alaior—Es Mercadal—Ferreries—Ciutadella *Línia 01, daily, from the bus station in Mahón and the Plaça de S'Esplanada in Ciutadella. Journey times: Alaior 15min, Es Mercadal 30min, Ferreries 45min, Ciutadella 1h15min*
Departs Mahón (weekdays) 08.15 and hourly until 22.15; (Sat/Sun/holidays) 08.00, 10.00, 11.30, 13.00, 16.00*, 16.30■, 18.00*, 19.00 21.30*
Departs Ciutadella (weekdays) 07.40 and hourly until 21.40; (Sat/Sun/holidays) 08.00, 10.00, 11.30, 14.30, 16.00*, 16.30■, 18.00*, 19.00, 20.00*, 21.30*

1A Mahón—Ciutadella express *Mon-Fri, from the bus station in Mahón. Journey time about 50min*
Dep Mahón 7.00, 8.00, 9.45, 10.45, 12.45, 14.15, 15.15, 16.45, 17.45, 19.45, 21.15
Dep Ciutadella 7.00, 8.00, 9.10, 11.15, 12.10, 14.15, 15.15, 16.15, 18.10, 19.10, 21.15

2 Mahón—Es Castell *Línia 02, daily, from the bus station in Mahón. Journey time 10min*
Departs Mahón 07.20*, 07.45*, 08.15*, 08.45*; half-hourly from 09.15 to 10.45; from 11.45 to 13.45, 14.15*, 14.45*, 15.15*; from 15.45 to 16.45; from 17.45 to 20.45
Departs Es Castell 07.30*, 08.00*, 08.30*, 09.00*; then half-hourly from 09.30 to 11.00; from 12.00 to 14.00; 14.30*, 15.00*, 15.30*; and from 16.00 to 21.00

3 Mahón—Sant Lluís *Línia 03, daily, from the bus station in Mahón. Journey time 10min*
Departs Mahón 07.15*, 08.10*, 08.30*; then hourly from 09.30 to 13.30; 15.15; hourly from 16.30 to 19.30; then 20.15
Departs Sant Lluís 07.30*, 08.20; then hourly from 09.50 to 12.50; 15.45; then hourly from 16.50 to 19.50

4 Mahón—Punta Prima *Línia 92, daily, from Mahón bus station. Journey time 25min*
Departs Mahón 07.00*, 08.00*; hourly from 09.00 to 13.00; 14.00*, 15.00*; hourly from 16.00-19.00; and finally at 20.00*, 21.00*, 22.00*, 23.00*; returns from Punta Prima (in front of Hotel Xaloc) 30 minutes later

5 Mahón—Alcaufar—S'Algar—Las Palmeras *Línia 91, daily, from Mahón bus station. Journey times: Alcaufar 15min, Las Palmeras 25min, S'Algar 30min*
Departs Mahón 08.30, 09.30, 12.30, 13.30, 15.30, 18.30; returns from S'Algar 30 minutes later

6 Mahón—Binibeca *Línia 93, daily, from Mahón bus station. Journey time 25min*
Departs Mahón 10.30, 14.20, 17.30; returns from Binibeca 11.00, 14.35, 18.00

7 Mahón—Sant Climent—Son Vitamina—Cala'n Porter *Línia 31, Mon-Sat from Mahón bus station. Journey times: Sant Climent 10min, Son Vitamina 15min, Cala'n Porter 20min*
Departs Mahón 09.30, 10.30, 11.45, 13.30, 16.00, 18.00, 19.40
Departs Cala'n Porter 10.00, 11.00, 12.15, 13.45, 16.30, 18.30, 20.00

8 Mahón—Es Grau *daily (July-Sept only), from Mahón bus station. Journey time 25min*
Departs Mahón 10.00, 11.00■, 12.00*, 13.00■, 17.00
Departs Es Grau 10.30, 11.30■, 12.30*, 13.30■, 17.30

9 Mahón—Alaior—Torre Solí-Nou—Club San Jaime—Son Bou *Línia 32, Mon-Sat, from Mahón bus station. Journey times: Alaior 10min, Torre Solí-Nou 25min, Club San Jaime/Son Bou 30min*
Departs Mahón 08.30, 10.00, 11.30, 13.00, 17.00, 18.30, 20.00; returns from Son Bou one hour later

*except Sun/holidays; ■ only on Sun/holidays

133

10 Mahón—Sant Tomàs *Linea 71, daily, from Mahón bus station. Journey time 45min*
Departs Mahón 08.00*, 08.15■, 10.15*, 11.15■, 12.30*, 14.15■, 15.15*, 17.30*,
18.30■, 19.45*; returns 50min later (Mon-Sat), 35min later (Sun/holidays)

11 Mahón—Arenal d'en Castell—Son Parc—Fornells *daily, from J A Clavé 7
(private bus company, not TMSA). Journey times: Arenal 30min, Son Parc 55min, Fornells
1h10min*
Dep Mahón 11.00, 13.00*, 19.00; Departs Fornells 08.30■, 09.00*, 15.45*, 17.00■
Dep Son Parc 15min later and Arenal 40min later

12 Mahón—Cala Santa Galdana *Linea 51, daily, from Mahón bus station. Journey time
45 minutes*
Departs Mahón 09.30*, 10.30■, 16.15*, 17.30■; returns about 50 minutes later

SERVICES TO AND FROM CIUTADELLA: see also (1 and 1A) above

13 Ciutadella—Sant Tomàs *Linea 72, daily from TMSA, Plaça dels Pins. Journey 1h*
Departs Ciutadella 08.00*, 10.15*, 11.40■, 12.30*, 14.40■, 15.15*, 17.30*, 18.30■,
19.45*
Departs Sant Tomàs 08.35*, 10.50*, 12.15■, 13.20*, 15.15■, 15.50*, 18.05*,
19.05■, 20.35*

14 Ciutadella—Santandría—Cala Blanca *daily** from Plaça de S'Esplanada. Journey
times: Santandría 10min, Cala Blanca 15min*
Departs Ciutadella 07.00, 08.00, 09.00, 09.40*, 10.10, 10.40*, 11.15, 11.50,
12.30*, 13.15, 13.45*, 14.15*, 14.45*, 15.15*, 16.00, 17.00*, 18.00, 19.00,
20.00*, 21.00, 22.20; returns from Cala Blanca about 25 minutes later

15 Ciutadella—Cala'n Bosch—Son Xoriguer *daily** from Plaça de S'Esplanada.
Journey times: Cala'n Bosch 15min, Son Xoriguer 20min*
Departs Ciutadella 07.00, 08.00, and from 08.45* to 14.30 every 15min (every
30min on Sundays); then 15.00 to 23.30 every 30min (every hour on the
half hour on Sundays); return times about 20 minutes later
Also **Cala Blanes—Cala'n Bosch** *daily:* Departs 09.10, 11.00; returns 12.45, 17.20
Also **Son Blanc—Cala'n Bosch** *daily:* Departs 10.15; returns 15.45
Also **Cala Blanca—Cala'n Bosch** *daily:* Departs 10.25; returns 15.45

16 Ciutadella—Cala Santa Galdana *Linea 52, daily, from TMSA, Plaça dels Pins.
Journey time about 30min.*
Departs Ciutadella 09.50■, 10.40*, 13.50, 16.45
Departs Cala Santa Galdana 10.00*, 10.20■, 13.20, 16.20*, 17.20■
Also **Ciutadella—Ferreries—Cala Santa Galdana** *Linea 53; see Timetable 19 below*

17 Ciutadella—Los Delfines—Cala Forcat *daily** from Plaça de S'Esplanada*
Departs Ciutadella 07.15*, 08.15*, 08.40, 09.05, 09.35*, 09.50, 10.05*, 10.30,
10.50*, 11.05, 11.30*, 11.55, 12.30*, 13.00, 13.30*, 14.00, 14.30*, 15.00*, 15.30,
16.00*, 16.30, 17.00*, 17.30, 18.00*, 18.30, 19.15, 20.00, 20.45; returns 10
minutes later

18 Ciutadella—Son Blanc—Sa Caleta *daily** from Plaça de S'Esplanada*
Departs Ciutadella 08.50, 10.10, 11.10*, 12.05, 13.00, 14.05*, 15.00*,
16.20, 17.30*, 18.30, 19.30, 20.30*; returns 5 minutes later

19 Ciutadella—Cala Morell *daily** from Plaça de S'Esplanada*
Departs Ciutadella 11.20, 15.15, 18.30; returns about 15 minutes later

SERVICES TO AND FROM FERRERIES (run by TMSA): see also (1) and (16) above

20 Ferreries—Cala Santa Galdana *Linea 53, daily. Journey time 15min. These connect
with the Mahón—Ciutadella—Mahón service (1).*
Departs Ciutadella 07.05*, 08.05*, 09.05, 09.40*, 10.05-13.05 hourly, 15.05*,
16.05, 16.50*, 17.05-20.05 hourly, 21.05*, 22.05*; returns 15 minutes later

*except Sun/holidays; ■ only on Sun/holidays; **service of the Torres bus company, with departures from the
Plaça de S'Esplanada